Introduction

There are many, many reasons I am happy about the publication of this book, not the least of which is that I don't have to Christmas shop this year.

But perhaps the biggest reason is that this book – which contains the best (or, depending on your viewpoint, the least objectionable) of my columns for The Flint Journal since I arrived here in November 1989 – gives me an opportunity to share credit/blame with people who deserve it.

These people include: Mike Riha, Journal metro editor, whose crackpot idea it was to hire me; Tom Lindley and Roger Samuel, editor and publisher of The Journal, who patiently stand behind me (sometimes way, WAY behind me) even when I write stuff that gets them in trouble; former Journal publisher Danny Gaydou, ditto; Cookie Wascha, my favorite boss; Jackie Braun, Jennifer Kildee and Kathy Greenfield, whose diligent editing saves me countless embarrassments; Rose Reiz, the perfect sounding board and all-around cool gal-pal; Dave Fenech, former Journal editorial department pooh-bah, whose encouragement sustained me; my wife, the lovely yet formidable Marcia, whose love, patience and ability to gently tell me "That sucks" mean more to me than I can ever tell her; my son, the loud and unruly Sam, who is not only my best buddy but great material; my family, who would never let me hear the end of it if I didn't mention them here; and of course you, the faithful and not so faithful readers of my column, whose taste in newspaper writers is questionable but deeply appreciated anyway.

Andrew S. Heller

To Mom and Dad

ISBN 0-9649832-1-4

Printed in the United States of America.

Edited by Cookie Wascha
Cover photograph by Steve Kleeman
Design by Jeff Johnston

First Edition

Contents

The Young and the Restless

Little Things

Follow the Bouncing Ball

U.P. Living

Life in the '90s

The Young and the Restless

'Stop that!' A preview of parenting

I am writing this at home. Or trying to. My nephew is staying with us for the weekend. He is 3½. This means I ...

"Stop that."

This means I am spending a lot of time trying to scold him. Not that he ever hears me. In the .0002 nanoseconds it takes the words to make it from my brain to my mouth, he is long gone, a 3-foot blur streaking through the house. If he didn't take naps I wouldn't know what he looks like.

I keep trying anyway. I say ...

"I said, stop that!"

I say things like, "You can have dessert if you finish your vegetables," and "Be careful! You could put somebody's eye out with that!"

I don't know where these phrases come from. They just pop out, like my mom always said they would. It's like some recessive parental nagging gene suddenly activated itself.

But then ...

"That! Stop that! ... because I said so!"

But then Marcia and I – I should mention here that we have been married for eight years but are still childless, by my choice, not hers – are learning all sorts of things about parenting this weekend.

First of all, we learned why, when Kyle's parents dropped him off on the way to their first no-kids getaway in two years, they arrived suspiciously early and stayed just long enough –

approximately four seconds – to deposit Kyle and roughly three tons of toddler paraphernalia inside the front door. As they sped off, we swear we heard laughter.

We also learned why ...

"Put that down."

Why when we visit our friends with young children at Christmas, the tree has ornaments only on the top half. Unfortunately, we learned this only after Kyle grabbed an antique tin toy off a shelf and turned it into origami.

That was yesterday. Today our house has been child-proofed. Nothing of any value, including the cat, has been left on any table or shelf below the 4-foot level. The place looks like it was decorated by very tall people.

We also learned that ...

"Go ask Aunt Marcia."

That if you take a child to Chuck E. Cheese's once, he will nag you to take him again and again and again until, finally, you reach the point where you find yourself saying, in all seriousness, "Chuck E. moved away."

"I SAID go ask your Aunt Marcia."

You also learn that 3½-year-olds are (pardon me, but it's true) booger factories. Unfortunately, I did not find this out until I picked up the control to the Nintendo game after Boogerboy had been playing.

I may touch it again. Someday.

So, with all this, you might think ...

"Kyle! Take that out of your mouth!"

You might think I would be happy to see Kyle go. That I would be counting every last tick of the remaining two hours, 15 minutes and 32 seconds before Kyle's parents are due to pick him up. *Au contrair.* In a way, I will be ...

"Plants are for looking at, not for eating!"

I will be sad to see the little bugger go. You see, Marcia wants kids. I want them, too, of course, just not yet. I had five siblings, and for years the instant I picked up a toy someone grabbed it away from me. Now that I am an adult, I want to keep my toys to myself, at least for a little while longer.

The problem is Marcia came from a small family, so naturally she wants to field her own baseball team. And she's been in the batter's box for years, if you catch my drift.

Normally, though, she's very good about not bringing up this topic more than 14 times a day. But I've noticed that ...

"But the doggy doesn't like it when you do that."

That since Kyle has been here, Marcia has been unusually silent on the topic, perhaps owing to the fact that, in a single weekend, we both have taken on the gaunt, exhausted, shell-shocked look common to only three types of people: bombardment victims, parents and baby-sitters.

So I don't mind having Kyle here. In fact, Marcia's been so silent about her biological clock that I may ...

"Kyle? Kyle? Honey, have you seen Kyle? It's awfully quiet."

I may invite him back next weekend.

Children. The ultimate birth control.

— *April 20, 1992*

After 10 years of pestering, we're pregnant

We're pregnant. Actually, she's pregnant. I am merely the accessory to the crime, as it were. Although it is a frightening idea. If men got pregnant, you can bet there'd be a whole lot more elbow room in the world.

Anyway, it happened in the normal way. She pestered me for 10 years about having kids and I finally relented.

Actually, that's not quite the truth. She wanted kids. I did not. And not because I don't like them, but because I've never fully abandoned the view of myself as a child, and, quite frankly, I wasn't ready to share my toys.

Fine by her. She was willing to wait, just not forever. So from time to time she would turn to me and say, "Tick," which was her way of reminding me that her biological alarm clock was running.

Not that I needed the reminding. I have a mother. Mothers are nature's way of ensuring the survival of the species.

"Aren't the two of you pregnant yet?" my mother has said to me at one point during just about every conversation we've had over the past decade.

Finally, a few months ago, Mom got her wish. Marcia's alarm went off like the bells of Notre Dame, and no matter how hard I tried, I couldn't find the snooze button.

Again, I'm teasing. It was a mutual decision. It was time, we figured, unless we wanted to someday be the only grandparents on the block sharing their grandchildren's baby food.

Although, I will admit that Marcia was a wee bit more, ahem, serious about the whole thing than I was.

How can I put this delicately? Remember the Pink Panther movies with Peter Sellers as Inspector Clouseau? And remember Kato, Clouseau's sidekick who was under orders to attack the great detective without warning?

I was Clouseau. She was Kato. Capish?

Strangely enough, this approach didn't work, not that Marcia was deterred. She bought a book and figured out the time of the month she was most likely to conceive. Then, when that moment arrived, she would call me on the phone at work.

"I'm ovvvvulaaaating!" she would say in a sing-songy voice.

And I would sigh, stop what I was doing and shuffle on home to do my duty, feeling somehow like Man-O-War in his stud years.

It did the trick, though. We are due in February, and everything is moving along just fine. Marcia has already picked out 10 names she likes, her mother has already rejected those 10 and has provided her with a suitable substitute list, which my mother has reviewed and summarily rejected.

We'll end up calling the kid X.

We're also busy telling our friends the good news. Of course, they're happy for us, but you can tell the childless friends are thinking, "You poor saps. You'll never dine out in peace again."

And the ones with children are thinking, "Aha! Payback time!" Boy, teach a few kids how to make underarm noises and some people never forgive you.

Needless to say, these friends will never meet my children.

Me? I'm thrilled. A son, a daughter, it doesn't matter which. In my mind, one has already signed to play shortstop for the Detroit Tigers and the other is a Supreme Court Justice. And Clarence Thomas better not offer her a Coke, if you know what I mean.

I'm also a little worried. Will I be a good father? Will I say the right things? Will I repeat my parents' sins and successes? And the big one – am I ready for this?

It's probably too late for that, though. Like fathers, life has a way of teaching you to swim by tossing you in the lake. Once you're in, there's no use worrying about being wet. Just paddle like hell and hope you're doing it right.

That doesn't make it any less scary. Change, especially when you've been childless adults for as long as we have, isn't easy.

The other day, for instance, we were driving in the car when a minivan full of children and smeared windows sped by. It had wood paneling on the side, just like my parent's station wagon, and one of those obnoxious "Baby on Board" signs stuck to the glass.

"You know," said Marcia, a grin breaking across her face. "There's one of those in our future."

A minivan? Me?

Hold me. I'm so afraid.

— July 18, 1993

Without sleep, life is a dream with new baby

I haven't slept in a week, my eyes look like cracked glass and gray hair is sprouting like dandelions on my head. I've been peed on, pooped on, drooled on, howled at and seen more 4 a.m.'s over the past seven days than I did during four effervescent years of college.

I couldn't be happier.

His name is Samuel Joseph. Samuel because we like the name. It sounds good and strong and guyish. And Joseph because he was conceived the day before my dad died last June, God rest his soul, and Joseph was his name.

We like the name. But Marcia's grandmother wrinkled her nose and said, "Samuel Joseph? What kind of a name is Samuel Joseph?"

We've gotten a lot of that. People are funny that way. But we understand. He doesn't seem like a Sam to us yet either. Names are like blue jeans. You have to wear them awhile before they fit right.

So Samuel Joseph it is. Not Sammy, not Sammy Joe, not Sam I Am, Green Eggs and Ham, not the Samster, not Sam the Man, all of which I've heard already.

Just Sam. Or Samuel. Call him anything else, I'll sic the dog on you. You've been warned.

His vital statistics are as follows:

Born: Saturday, Feb. 26, 6:40 a.m. It's an unwritten law that children do not arrive during hours in which their parents are normally awake. This is nature's way of training parents for sleepless nights to come.

Height: 20½ inches.

Weight: 7 pounds even, although Marcia will tell you it felt more like 27.

Attractiveness quotient: Ruggedly handsome in a cute sort of way, if I do say so myself. And I do. They say all new babies look like Winston Churchill, but in our case that isn't true. He looks more like Yul Brynner.

Throws: A fit, usually. Although his throwing arm has potential, which is good because his dad is counting on him playing shortstop for the Detroit Tigers someday. Not that I intend to be one of those obnoxious, unyielding sports parents. Not at all. If he wants to be a *pitcher* for the Tigers, that's fine, too.

Sleeps: Never, as far as we can tell.

Lungs: Fine. Believe me. Very strong. The kid's another Pavarotti.

Mother's Condition: Great. Walking funny. But great.

Father's Condition: Amazed, daunted, grateful, educated. Watching Marcia, I learned three things. First, never correct a woman in labor. At one point I said, "Uh, honey, I don't think you're supposed to be panting here, you're supposed to be ... ."

She grabbed me by the collar and hissed in a voice straight out of "The Exorcist," "I'll breathe any (bleeping) way I wanna breathe, got it?" And then her head spun all the way around. Spooky.

Second, it's a good thing I'm a man because I don't think I'd have the courage or strength to give birth to a child. If women can do that, they sure as heck can run the country. So get off Hillary's back, all right?

Third, doctors are sneaky. They'll wait until the baby is born, then ask if you want to cut the cord. Cut the cord? I'm having trouble staying vertical here and she wants me to perform a medical procedure? What is this, self-serve medicine? And if I screw up, do I sue myself for malpractice? I said no.

A quick cord story: My brother looked down as his wife was delivering a few years ago, saw his child's head appear, then the shoulders, then the cord, at which point he joyously exclaimed, "It's a boy!"

It was a girl. The cord fooled him. We may let him forget that story 20 or 30 years from now.

Anyway, Samuel is ours. We've said that to ourselves over and over again.

"We did that," we say, looking down at him in wonder, amazed that the two of us could produce something so utterly beautiful.

"We did that," we say, holding him in our arms and thanking the Lord for bringing him into this world safely, with all his fingers, toes and whatnots.

"We did that," we say, momentarily stunned by the awesome lifetime responsibility – no four-year leases here – this creature before us represents.

"We did that," we whisper when he coos like a dove and turns our hearts to butter.

And then he soils his diaper and we look at one another and say, "YOU do that. It's your turn."

That's pretty much the parenthood experience as I see it so far. One minute the child is a gift from on high and the next he's doing something that drives you nuts, but in a way it's OK because, hey, he's your kid.

A comedian put it best. He said, "It's a good thing kids are cute. Otherwise we'd kill them."

Bingo.

Welcome to the world, Samuel Joseph. Your weary parents think you're pretty swell.

Now go to sleep, wouldja?

— *March 10, 1994*

Sam's tips on training humanoids

All was quiet. I was on the couch. My wife was on the love seat. Sam, our 8-month-old son, was on the floor, patiently ripping a Newsweek to shreds.

Suddenly, an air-raid siren went off. Or maybe it was the baby. Sometimes it's hard to tell. Either way, it sounded like this: "EEEEEEEE!" And then he looked at us, giggled and quietly resumed his original destruction.

"What was that all about?" I asked Marcia.

"Who knows," she replied. "There's a book out now that says men are from Mars and women are from Venus. Maybe babies are from Pluto."

We laughed then but we are not laughing now.

Oh, no. Not since the memo. I found it tucked under the mattress of Sam's crib. I read it and my blood ran cold:

To: The home planet

From: Agent XB49, aka "Sam."

Re: Progress report, Operation Soften Up.

Am posing as a humanoid infant and continuing subjugation/conditioning training of assigned adult humanoids per pre-invasion plans. They suspect nothing.

Began process of breaking wills of assigned parental units through recommended method of sleep-deprivation. Subjects, however, were tough zermdacs to crack. Awakening them with anguished roof-lifting howls every three hours, according to procedure 14-P55, failed to produce satisfactory deterioration of mental and physical abilities.

Agent therefore decided to step up effort to every hour and a half and maintained same for six months, at which point humanoids began displaying signs of severe debilitation.

Recently, the male humanoid – clearly the weaker of the two – broke into tears at 3 a.m., pleading piteously with me in the following manner: "For the love of God, go to sleep, wouldja? Daddy and Mommy are turning into zombies. And you don't want zombies for parents, do ya, pal? Huh?"

Other techniques used:

• Indiscriminate crying. Humanoids seem particularly vulnerable to this form of will-breaking. This agent has learned that a well-placed yowl – whether there is anything wrong or not – will bring both parental units running, thus breaking them of the belief that they are in charge of their lives.

• Scatological dominance. Another recommended technique for showing humanoids, as they say on this planet, "who is the boss." For maximum effect, agent suggests refilling diaper nanoseconds after a fresh one is applied.

• Food refusal. Few methods are as effective at eliciting the frustration response in adult humanoids as refusing to ingest consumables. Pretending to ingest consumables and then ejecting them forcefully onto curtains, walls, humanoids etc. is also a recommended strategy.

• Territorial markings. Female humanoid complained recently: "All of my clothes have spit-up, boogers (note: humanoid slang for nasal emissions) or drool on the shoulders. I'm not a woman anymore, I'm a grunge sponge." Marking one's humanoids in such a manner is a wise idea, as it gets them used to the idea of becoming another being's property.

To conclude, all is well. By the designated invasion date, assigned humanoids should be whimpering puddles of sleepy indecision, easily subdued and enslaved. Hope other agents are having similar success.

Hail to the Leader.

— November 7, 1994

New vehicle confirms worst fears

I find myself thinking the same thing over and over.

I own a minivan.

I own a minivan.

I own a minivan.

Sometimes I examine this thought with the sort of curious, shocked detachment one experiences after suffering a major body wound. Other times I'm a tad less cerebral:

"AAAAAAAAAH! I OWN A MINIVAN! MY LIFE IS OVER! MY DAD HAS TAKEN CONTROL OF MY BODY! SOMEBODY HELP ME! I'M TOO YOUNG FOR THIS!"

Because, like most guys, I guess I thought that a minivan – the station wagon of the '90s – would never happen to me. My mental image of myself, as it relates to things vehicular, is more along the line of the Madison Avenue stereotype.

I am shoehorned behind the wheel of a red convertible, driving along a winding California coast road on the way to everywhere and nowhere. Next to me is a dazzling blonde with a dangerous reputation, and we are laughing out loud about a very sophisticated joke as the wind wiggles our hair.

"Happy, darling?" she asks, placing a manicured hand on my thigh.

"Oh, yes, my sweet. Very."

Now here's reality. I am behind the wheel of a silver, used minivan driving along a city street with more holes in it than Dan Rostenkowski's alibi, and we are on the way to the grocery store to buy extra-absorbent diapers (our 3-month-old son being a urinary overachiever).

Next to me is a dazzling blonde with a dangerous look on her face. She is trying to calm the baby, who is in the back screaming so energetically that motorists are veering off the road in anticipation of an emergency vehicle.

The blonde glares at me and says: "If you hadn't honked at that guy who cut you off the baby would still be asleep. You happy now?"

"Oh, yes, my sweet," I say, gripping the wheel harder. "Very."

We bought the minivan several weeks ago. It is "her" car, replacing the one she'd had for years that gave up the ghost – this is no lie – the very day we paid off "my" car. Marcia calls this a "coincidence." I call it "suspiciously convenient." (Picture her under the hood of her car, ripping wires while humming the jingle of the local minivan dealership).

I had one simple rule: No wood-grain paneling. My dad once bought a station wagon with wood-grain paneling, and we cool-conscious kids about went into shock. The "geekmobile" we called it, if I recall.

That's the scary part about minivans to many guys. They are what our dads would buy if they were family men today, and none of us wants to turn into our dads, no matter how great they were.

Sure, we know it's going to happen sooner or later anyway, but there's no sense rushing things. After all, it's a short step from buying minivans to grumbling about the tripe that teenagers are listening to these days and fretting publicly about one's colon.

Marcia insisted, though. She said we need more room for the baby. My response was, "How much room could one little baby require?"

If you can't tell, this is our first child. Otherwise I would not have made such a patently absurd statement. Babies themselves don't require much space. Their equipment, however, is another matter. Babies, I have learned, travel about as lightly as your average Army battalion.

Not only that, their stuff, I am beginning to suspect, breeds. We went on an out-of-town trip recently, and I swear we came back with more baby paraphernalia than we had when we left, which may explain the heavy breathing I heard way in the back.

After all my griping, you may be wondering at this point how I like the minivan. The answer is ... I love it.

After years of staring up at other drivers from the cockpit of my ground-hugging compact, I am actually above most of the traffic now. I no longer feel like a 2-year-old staring at the knees of the adults around him.

Plus there is something cool about the driver's compartment – the swivel captain's chair, the controls and switches spread in an arc before me. When I drive this thing, I feel like James T. Kirk of the starship Enterprise. ("Scottie! We need warp speed in two seconds or we miss the yellow!")

And of course the extra space is nice.

So, really, the only drawback I see to this minivan thing is that it's only a matter of time before hair starts sprouting in my ears and I begin griping about the government.

And can anyone tell me why I have this sudden urge to buy more life insurance?

— June 12, 1994

Differences separate dads and fathers

Dear Sam:

This is my first Father's Day, so naturally people have been asking me all week how I like being a daddy.

I've been telling them I don't know.

See, I don't consider myself a full-fledged daddy yet.

I'm a father. And in my mind, there's a big difference.

We'll have this talk later on, but a father is someone who merely plants the seed that mothers use to bring children into the world. A daddy is someone who nurtures those children as they grow.

We'll see how I do at that. As for the seed thing, well, I'm certainly guilty of that, despite all the dumb jokes your mom and I endured about the mailman, the pizza delivery boy, *et al.*

I'm also guilty of taking my sweet time about it. You arrived just shy of four months ago, a whopping 10 years after I married your mom.

Our friends considered that a long time to go childless. They teased me about how I should take vitamin pills or get an instruction manual.

You'll understand someday.

Anyway, we waited so long because I wasn't ready. When a guy grows up with four brothers and a sister, he wants some time to himself.

Plus, you've got to be responsible and grown up to be a good dad, and I always felt like too much of a kid.

There was always one more trip I wanted to go on, one more ballgame to play, one more something I just had to do. And to be honest, I always thought fatherhood would mean the end of all that.

So I put your mother off. I think that made her a little sad. She wanted you in the worst way.

She would tell me all the time that her biological alarm clock was ringing and that I'd better shut it off or she'd find someone who would.

I think she was kidding, but a guy can't be too sure.

So, finally we had you, on a blizzardy night in February.

Your mom was in labor (an accurate word if ever there was one) throughout the big Olympic skating finals.

We would watch that little cur Tonya Harding for a while, then your mom would moan for awhile.

I'd joke that she should pipe down so I could hear the commentator. Your mom didn't think that was funny. But you'll learn that your dad has a weird sense of humor.

Finally, about 4 a.m., you indicated you were about ready to make your debut, so we mushed to the hospital through a foot of snow.

You were born at 6:40 a.m.

Like my dad, I'm not a crier. I remember crying three times in my life: when I slid into a picker bush we were using as first base when I was 5; when your grandpa died last June (Lord, how I wish you had met him); and when I held you for the first time.

But I couldn't help it. You were so small and so beautiful.

So I blubbered away.

Don't tell anyone, OK?

I also remember thinking, "My god, I'm a daddy," and being struck by what an awesome responsibility that is.

Marriages you can leave.

Jobs you can quit.

Cars you can trade in.

Pets you can give away.

But this parent stuff, it's a lifetime deal. You commit to parenthood, you commit yourself forever.

At least that's the way it's supposed to be. Sadly, that's not the way it actually is too often these days.

That's what I mean about the difference between being a father and a daddy.

Fathers are there at the beginning. Dads are there all the time.

Fathers are too busy to play catch. Dads put down the paper and play catch even when they don't feel like it.

Fathers are quick with discipline. Dads count to 10, then decide what's best.

Fathers insist that their word is law. Dads consider things from the kid's perspective.

Fathers let Mom handle most of the emotional stuff. Dads laugh and cry with their children.

And last but not least, fathers believe the mere biological act qualifies them as dads. True dads understand that theirs is a title bestowed upon them by their children.

In other words, you earn it.

And I haven't yet.

So to get back to the original question, I don't know yet how I like being a daddy.

I can tell you this, though, kiddo:

I'm looking forward to finding out.

Love, Your Father/Dad

—June 19, 1994

Son's surgery giving Dad, Mom pains

Tomorrow morning we take Sam, our son, in for surgery. He's just 16 months old, younger than the bottle of hot sauce in our refrigerator, so he has no idea what's coming.

His mother and I, though, know all too well.

And we, frankly, are utter wrecks: Our son? Under hot lights? Under anesthesia? Under the care of strangers?

It's not an easy thing to contemplate, no matter how minor the procedure.

And it is minor. That is what we've been told and what we keep telling ourselves: It's minor, it's minor, it's minor. We say this with the wan smiles of the unconvinced.

The problem is this: He was born tongue-tied. This means that when he attempts to stick out his tongue, the tip curls under, like a pink wave. Right now it's no problem. He can manipulate food correctly, and that's what's most important.

The problem may lie down the road, with his speech. He may have trouble forming some sounds, and speech therapy may be necessary. This is a benign enough thing, but we, like all parents, want our son to be perfect.

A close friend of ours has had an attached tongue all her life. It's no big deal now, she says. Still, she wishes her parents had done for her what we're doing for Sam.

She was teased, she remembers, because she couldn't stick out her tongue like the other kids, couldn't curl it into a little tunnel and suck down spaghetti; couldn't catch snowflakes with the tip of it; was embarrassed to kiss on dates when she got older.

We don't want our son to be teased. We want him to slurp spaghetti. We want him to catch snowflakes. We don't want him to be embarrassed. We want him to do all the rude, dumb, wonderful things kids do with their tongues. But most of all, we want his speech to develop normally.

And so we're going ahead with it.

They tell us it's a simple procedure. They give him a shot that "makes him happy." (How about one for his parents?) Then they administer a general anesthesia so he doesn't struggle. They they open his mouth and snip the fibrous tissue restraining the tip of his tongue. The whole thing, start to finish, will take 20 minutes, and he'll be home within a few hours. In my mind, though, it will seem like 20 years.

I have to struggle to restrain the panic just to write this. I keep imagining not what could go right, but what could go wrong. Don't they make you sign those awful forms? The ones larded with legalistic mumbo-jumbo that say, in essence: "Nothing should go wrong, nothing will go wrong ... but you never know."

When I imagine him on that table, limp and dreaming, strangers in masks holding sharp things above him, without us there to protect him, well it's almost more than I can bear.

I mean, this is my son. We waited 10 years to have him. We wanted to be ready, wanted it to be right, and now he's here and it is. He is a wonderful, wonderful boy. Sometimes when I look at him and I see his smile and the light in his young eyes, I love him so much it hurts.

I realize how trite this sounds, but I don't care, just as I don't care how dumb and corny it sounds when we say that we would happily take his place on the table if we could.

Because we would. In a heartbeat. Like any parent.

The problem, of course, is that we can't. So tomorrow morning we will do something much more painful. We will take our son, our Sam, to surgery.

He'll be fine. We're sure of it.

Us? That's another matter entirely.

— July 30, 1995

Dad-to-be gets earful from old pro

A friend of mine is going to have a child soon.

Actually, he isn't going to have the child. She will have the child. He will probably pass out in the delivery room. But you know what I mean.

Anyway, since I am a new father and an expert on the process by which babies are brought into the world, it's only natural that my friend came to me for advice.

"I'm a little frightened about the delivery," he said. "Do I have to go?"

"Of course you have to go," I reply. "These are the '90s."

"So?"

"So if you try to sit around the waiting room cracking jokes and handing out cigars like fathers used to do, the mother will sic hospital security on you and they'll drag you in anyway. So you might as well make it easy on yourself and go in voluntarily."

"I had no idea."

"And once you're in there, there's no use faking an illness or pretending you have to make a phone call or use the toilet."

"Why not?"

"Because I tried it and it doesn't work. If I recall, my wife's exact words when I tried to sneak out were 'Get back here, you %¢$@! coward!' "

"My, my, such profanity."

"Women in labor aren't known for their restraint."

"But, look," my friend protested, a concerned look on his face, "I can't go in there. I can't stand the sight of blood."

"Neither can I," I replied, patting his shoulder. "That's why I didn't watch. I remember it clearly. While the doctor was working on the south end of my wife, I kept my eyes glued squarely on the north."

"That sounds sensible. But what if the doctor asks if you want to cut the cord? I hear they do that nowadays."

"Yes, they do. And when the doctor asked me I said, 'Noooooo thank you, ma'am!' The way I figured it was, with my eyes closed, I was likely to slip with the scalpel and cut off the doctor's finger, and then she could sue me for malpractice."

"Good point. But what about my wife? I don't know if I can bear to see her in such pain."

"Don't worry," I said. "You'll be in far too much pain yourself to notice."

"What do you mean?"

"I mean that if she's anything like my wife, when a severe contraction hits, her head will spin around several times, like that girl in the 'Exorcist,' and she will grab whatever part of you is closest to her and squeeze it until you're singing in the soprano section of the choir on Sunday, if you know what I mean."

"That sounds horrible."

"It is. But think of it as her way of allowing you to experience the joy of birth that she is experiencing."

"Well, OK. But is there some way I can comfort my wife?"

"Breathe."

"You mean help her do all that huffing and puffing they teach you in Lamaze class?"

"No, I mean try to breathe normally yourself, because after you hear all that yelling and screaming and see all the gush and goo, you'll feel like passing out."

"Is there anything else I can do for her?"

"Well, some women appreciate having a focal point – something on which they can focus their attention so as not to notice that they are about to pass a bowling ball out of their lower regions."

"Did your wife have a focal point?" he asked.

"She did, indeed," I replied. "It was my nose, which was an inch from hers at the time. Late in labor, she grabbed me by the neck, drew my face to hers and hissed, 'You! You did this to me! I ... want ... you ... dead!' And then her head spun around a few more times."

"Birth sounds awful."

"Well, it's no picnic." I said, nodding sagely. "But remember, if things get too intense, there are always drugs."

"For my wife?"

"No, you ninny. For you."

— January 18, 1995

Little guy's word choice stuns public

We have reached the watch-what-you-say stage at my house.

This is the stage when your son, who is nearly 2, suddenly begins to repeat stuff you say. But only the bad stuff. That's what I don't get. Somehow he is able to sift through the 2,000 or so inoffensive words we might use during a typical day and zero in on the three or four bad ones.

It's an amazing ability. And now that he's learned it there's no getting him to knock it the hell off. (Heck. I mean heck. Gotta get used to that.)

For instance, my wife, the lovely yet formidable Marcia, was carrying a plate of bread to the dining table when she stumbled and dropped it.

"Oh, (bad word)," she blurted.

Now, before I go any further, I should note – since the lovely yet formidable Marcia says I have to – that she is not exactly a truck stop waitress in the swearing department. Usually she reserves her infrequent bursts of colorful language for when I forget to flush or when I get Cheetos dust on the new couch while watching three football games in a row.

Anyway, most of you will be able to figure out what she actually said, but in case you can't here's a hint: Newt Gingrich is full of it.

So to get on with this, naturally our son, the myna bird,

who was in his high chair, immediately chirped "(Bad word)!"

Then, somehow sensing that here was a word that he absolutely, positively should never, ever use again, he babbled it over and over.

"(Bad word)! (Bad word)! (Bad word)!" he beamed, throwing a spoonful of mashed potatoes at the cat for emphasis.

Marcia was, of course, horrified. And I, being the supportive husband that I am, immediately demonstrated enormous empathy for her dismay by laughing so hard I nearly choked on a carrot. She glared at me, but I said, "Oh, come on, don't worry, he doesn't even know what he said. I doubt he'll ever say it again."

Have I mentioned this is our first child? I say that because OF COURSE he said it again. All you veteran parents know that. You also probably know that he did not say it again right away. No, he cleverly bided his time, waiting for just the right moment, the right moment being defined as a moment causing maximum public embarrassment for his mother and father.

This moment came at the grocery store checkout.

"(BAD WORD)!" he shouted as the clerk ran a carton of milk across the scanner. Heads turned three lanes away.

"(BAD WORD)! (BAD WORD)! (BAD WORD)!"

People laughed understandingly, but Marcia was aghast.

"Must've picked that up in day care," she muttered to the clerk, a hand clamped over Sam's mouth.

"But he's not in day care," I added, helpfully.

I'll stop paying for that one sometime next millennium.

Anyway, since that incident we've definitely been much more careful with our language.

We've even come up with a George Carlin list. Remember? Carlin is the comedian with the famous bit about the seven words you can't say (or couldn't back then, anyway) on TV.

Only our list has two dozen words and phrases you can't say around Sam without paying for it later on.

It's sort of embarrassing, actually. I didn't know we knew that many bad words. But I guess we'll stick to this list at least until Sam is in high school.

At which point, I'm sure, he'll be able to teach us a few things.

—Jan. 15, 1996

Toddler's mayhem has alien touch

To: The Home Planet.

From: Agent XB49, aka "Sam."

Re: Progress report, Operation Soften Up.

Greetings, High Commander. Am continuing to pose as a humanoid 2-year-old. Surveillance and conditioning of assigned adult humanoids per pre-invasion plans proceeding smoothly. Currently am testing and observing humanoid response to physical and emotional stress through the following series of mystifying behaviors:

1) Object insertion. Humanoids seem easily panicked by any attempt by agent to insert nonconsumable objects – stones, earrings, pocket change, plant leaves, canine yard offerings – into agent's "mouth."

Typical female humanoid response: "No, no! Ucky ucky! Stop, stop!"

Typical male humanoid response: "What the hell ...?!"

Strongly suggest you equip invasion forces with numerous such items.

Note: Stress response is elicited nearly as well when humanoids observe consumable items known as "peas" being inserted in other cranial orifices (i.e. nostrils, ears).

2) Climbing. When humanoids aren't looking, agent repeatedly attempts to scale large objects such as dressers, bookshelves, etc.

Most recently, agent climbed atop the back of a humanoid

comfort device known as a "sofa," grabbed the pull cords for the window blinds and was ready to swing Tarzan-style onto nearby love seat when humanoids burst into room, eyes bugging out and legs spinning in the fashion of animated cathode-ray tube characters.

Female humanoid response: "No, no! Bad, bad! Stop, stop!"

Male humanoid response: "What the hell ...?!"

As you can see, humanoid response to stress follows a predictable pattern, a useful bit of knowledge indeed.

3) Back-seat screaming. It is this agent's recommendation that invasion forces engage in frenzied and persistent vocalizations at varying pitches, volumes and octaves, as this behavior seems to confuse and befuddle humanoids.

After a three-hour automobile trip, during which agent employed this technique the whole time (except when ingesting fried potato sticks from a roadside consumables establishment), the male humanoid was heard to mutter darkly to the female humanoid, "Never again. Never, ever again. Not in a million damn years. No trips over two minutes long, not unless we get him a %$@* muzzle."

Female humanoid did not respond, as her face was apparently stuck to her hands.

4) Constant mobility. Nowhere else is the difference between our two life forms more clearly evident than in physical endurance. Adult humanoids tire to the point of tongue-lolling a mere 20 hours into their 24-hour solar cycles, whereas agent is able to maintain an energetic pace for up to 36 hours before requiring seven minutes of what humanoids call "sleep."

Adult humanoids, by comparison, require a full five hours of sleep, and even then they are sluggish and prone to exasperation, as evidenced by the male humanoid's repeated and apparently unflattering comparison of this agent to "that freaking battery bunny." Agent has no idea what this means.

Conclusion: Humanoid tolerance for physical and emotional stress is laughably low. Domination and subjugation of this species should pose no particular problem but will administer further stress tests, as instructed.

Question: What is "potty training"?

— July 8, 1996

Little Things

Coffee mugs reveal a lot about owners

I have a new coffee mug in my life.

This is no small thing. It is quite a large thing, in fact.

It holds a half-cup more coffee than my old mug. This is good because the coffee czar here at the newspaper charges by the mug, not by how how much the mug holds.

I know a good deal when I see one.

It was love at first sight. Our food editor got the mug in the mail and thought it was disgusting so he put it out on a counter. And there it sat, waiting for someone to claim it.

No one did. This is probably because the word "Beano" is imprinted in big, green letters across it. Above it, in small black letters is, "Don't forget the ..."

Beano is a gas medicine. You pour a couple of drops on your food and you no longer have to blame it on the dog.

It's a funny name for a funny problem, so you can see why no one wanted the mug. Who wants to walk around the office carrying such a thing? It's almost like saying, "Don't get too close. I have an embarrassing problem."

Some people could take the message wrong, too. They see the words, "Don't forget the Beano" coming at them and they might think, "Is he/she trying to tell me something?"

It's an uncomfortable thing any way you look at it.

So who would want such a mug?

Well. Me. I'm sure that says something about me.

No. Not that. I have a dog.

I think it means that I like attention. Carry a Beano mug and attention is yours. It's like carrying a parrot on your shoulder. Or walking with a limp. Or wearing a halter top (again, this is not something I personally do).

Do any of those things and you will get plenty of attention. (Which, of course, is why people do them.)

Plus, it's time. By this I mean it is time for a new coffee mug. For five years I have used a White Castle coffee mug. White Castle is a burger chain. They make teeny-weeny burgers that many people call "sliders" because they are so greasy. I love sliders. One day I bought a bag of sliders and got the mug for a buck extra. Another good deal.

This mug has served me well. Once, when I was somewhere else in the building, I put the mug down and forgot to pick it up again. Naturally, I couldn't remember where I'd left it. I was heartbroken. Coffee didn't taste the same out of the mug I used as a substitute. It wasn't bad. It was just ... different.

So when I finally stumbled across my White Castle mug weeks later, I was elated. It was like finding a lost dog.

No, that's not funny. Ask any coffee drinker. He or she will tell you that you can become quite attached to your mug. Your mug is your friend, your enabler. Some people have a photo of their child transferred onto a mug. Others have mugs so old you could carbon-date the coffee stains.

Many people have mugs that don't look like anything special. But ask if you can borrow it and they act as if you are trying to kidnap their child.

A mug is a personal thing. There is history there. A person-mug relationship is often a good bet to last longer than a person-person relationship.

But, like any relationship, things can change.

You know how it is. You're cruising through life together. Everything's fine. Then, one day, I don't know, the zip just isn't there anymore. And soon you're looking, even if you're not completely aware that you're looking.

It happened to me. One day, there it was. The Beano mug. And I simply had to have it. Consequences be hanged.

I am such a disloyal pig.

But I have a new mug.

— December 4, 1994

Manuals written for idiot in us

I have been thinking for days about my wife's new curling iron. I have decided that it says a lot about our society. What it says mostly is this: "We are stupid."

There is no other explanation. Look at the instruction manual: "Use this appliance for its intended use as described in this manual."

Think about that for a moment. It means that there are people out there who actually use curling irons for other purposes. But what? You could, I suppose, use a curling iron to turn straight strands of dull, ordinary spaghetti into sophisticated, curlicue pasta. And a curling iron, in the wrong hands, would be a devilish form of torture ("Tell me the code or I'll give you SUCH a wave.").

Other than that I'm stumped.

Someone is obviously doing something with them other than hair curling, otherwise why would the company bother with such a warning?

Or this one: "Do not use ... where oxygen is being administered."

Oxygen? How many iron lung patients are worried about stylish hair?

Or this: "Never use while sleeping."

You might think, well, that's impossible. If you're asleep, you're asleep. You can no more curl your hair in your sleep than you can brush your teeth while comatose.

Ah, but people walk in their sleep, don't they? Maybe there are sleep curlers out there. Or maybe someone wrapped a hunk of hair around the curling iron, plugged it in and went beddy-bye thinking that by the time they awoke they'd have a curl strong enough to hang curtains on, an Annette Funicello-type curl.

No, I can't imagine doing this sort of thing, but then I am sane. That doesn't mean others wouldn't try it, though. I personally have seen a man try to trim his hedges with his lawn mower. (And it worked.)

And men will use anything as a hammer – firearms, beer bottles, small pets. My brother cleans carburetor parts in the dishwasher. My sister has been known to use a stapler for emergency hemming. And who hasn't tried drying underwear in the microwave?

People are nuts. That's why companies have to think up all these weirdo ways in which people might misuse a product and then put warnings against doing so in the instruction manual.

For instance, I recently bought a little desk fan. Under "special notes" in the instruction manual it says: "Do not use gasoline, alcohol, insecticide or any volatile chemicals to wash it."

Now, again, I would not do this. I would not think: "Hmm, I don't seem to have any soap to wash this here fan with. I wonder if some mosquito repellant or some unleaded petroleum would do the trick?"

But the company obviously felt the idea was likely to dawn on someone.

Or this: "Never insert fingers, pencils or any other object through the guard when fan is in operation."

You might wonder what kind of an idiot would do that?

But try to think like the manufacturer here: Your product has spinning blades and will be sitting on desks across America. People sitting at desks are often bored. And when they're bored, they notice things, such as their fingernails need clipping and their pencils need sharpening. And you just know there are never fingernail clippers or pencil sharpeners around when you need them.

So the only alternative is to use your fan! Yes! It's only logical!

Companies, of course, think like this for a reason. If they warn you not to do something with their product and you go ahead and do it anyway, they figure they're safe from lawsuits, though this isn't always the case.

Recently, for instance, a woman was awarded umpteen million dollars because she spilled McDonald's coffee on her hand, despite the fact that it was labeled "hot" right there on the lid. (An aside: I personally felt she should get more, as anyone who drinks the stuff knows that calling McDonald's coffee "hot" is an understatement of the highest order, sort of like calling Rush Limbaugh "somewhat irritating.")

Or let's go back to the curling iron, which came with the warning; "This curler is hot when in use."

Well, duh. Who doesn't know that a curling iron is hot?

But here's the key – and, really, the beautiful part about living in a nation like ours: If someone is stupid enough to not know that a curling iron gets hot when you plug it in, then surely they're too stupid to read the instructions.

And right there they have you: Lawsuit City.

Stupidity has its rewards.

— October 20, 1994

Milk crates shelved for real thing

Slowly, life takes away a guy's milk crates. I lost four more the other day. Marcia hauled them off to the basement after we bought bookshelves. Real bookshelves. Made out of real wood. Grown-up bookshelves.

We spent $250 on them, and they look great in the study, although our collection of paperbacks suddenly looks awfully shabby. And they do hold books, these bookshelves.

Just not any better than my plastic milk crates. Milk crates hardly cost anything at all. If you spent $250 on milk crates, you would run out of books to store long before you ran out of milk crates to store them in.

Frankly, I prefer the milk crates. They are functional and practical. And so is my wife, which is why I don't understand her objection to them.

"We are adults, and adults don't use milk crates," is all she says.

When she says this she means adult women. Adult men would probably use milk crates their entire lives if their wives and girlfriends let them, just as we would continue to wear our old underwear with the holes in it.

Women civilize men in many ways, which is good. And I'm glad Marcia is here to civilize me. If I didn't have her, I would still be eating pizza four nights a week in my underwear. At least now I leave my clothes on.

Sometimes, though, she moves too fast. I've had those milk crates a long time. Some of them I've had longer than I've had Marcia. You get rid of something like that, you lose a piece of your history.

"They're just plastic," she said. "I think you'll survive."

Easy for her to say. Unlike men, women fail to see the beauty of milk crates. Milk crates are functional and strong, just like men, and they come in a rainbow of attractive primary colors, and therefore fit any decor.

Milk crates never break, either. At least I've never broken one. You can leave wet glasses on them and they won't stain. You can put your feet on them and no one cares. You can be as neglectful of milk crates as you want, and they will never complain or let you down. Milk crates are the furniture equivalent of dogs.

In my college days, all the guys owned at least a half dozen. They held books, underwear, socks, empty beer bottles. They served as shelves, chairs, basketball hoops, wastebaskets, etc.

Where we got them, I don't remember. OK, I do remember, but I'm not going to tell you, because I'm not certain if there's a statute of limitations on that sort of thing.

I feel bad about it, really. The local dairies used to get the college paper to run articles from time to time saying that stealing milk crates was a crime that greatly increased the cost of milk and threatened to bring down the Republic.

We just laughed. We were that sort. Rogues. Free spirits. Bad boys. We even ripped the labels off of our pillows and mattresses. God help us.

Today, I understand, college students don't have to steal milk crates. Companies actually sell the things, which somehow doesn't seem as cool. More honest, but not as cool.

Anyway, when I left school my crates left with me. They saw Marcia and me through our pre-VISA years.

We had an entire entertainment center built out of milk crates. We stacked, if I remember, eight or nine of the things. On this edifice went our tiny TV, our tiny stereo system, our LPs and even a few plants.

We were so proud of it. It went so well with the electrical spool we turned into a coffee table and the stained futon we used for a couch.

In those days, we could not have lived without milk crates. That's the thing about time, though. Milk crates don't change, but people do.

Slowly, as our income grew, Marcia's fondness for milk crates waned. She would bring home a stereo stand or an end table, and another milk crate would end up in the basement. You can't stand in the way of progress or a woman with a decorating idea.

Now that we have real bookshelves, there are only three milk crates left in the house. All of them are in my study. One I turn over and use as a footstool.

The other two? They hold books that are too big for our fancy schmancy, store-bought, real-wood bookshelves.

I smile when I think of that.

— November 16, 1992

Choosing toothbrush a headache

The problem with America today is that there are too many choices.

I went to the store the other day and it took me 15 minutes to choose a toothbrush. Fifteen minutes! But what could I do? There was an entire section devoted to nothing but toothbrushes, all of them with different features.

And I didn't want to just grab any old brush, because, you know, what if it wasn't the right one for me? You don't want to buy a brush that isn't right for you because then you're stuck with it. You can't just throw it away because toothbrushes are expensive these days. And so every time you brush your teeth for the next three months, you're going to think, "You boob, you should have gone with the angled head!"

And who needs that? Not me, so I stood there and I studied my options.

First I looked for "boy" toothbrushes. You are probably not consciously aware of the fact that there are boy and girl toothbrushes, but it's true.

You can tell which is which by the colors. The girl brushes are pink, yellow and light blue and the boy brushes are ruby red, ocean blue and emerald green. Men are particularly picky about color. You will often see a woman choose a boy-color brush, but you will never see a man choose a girl-color brush. And if a woman buys a man a brush that's the wrong color, he may use it, but he won't like it, and he'll use every excuse to get rid of it.

"Whup!" he'll say. "Dropped it in the toilet. Guess I'll have to buy another one."

Next I looked for the proper head. Used to be, heads, as they say, was heads. There was nothing fancy about them. Just a piece of plastic with some bristles stuck to it.

Not any more. Now toothbrush heads are high science. There are diamond-shaped heads and angled heads and heads that vary in size. There'll probably be a two-headed brush soon, so busy people can cut their brushing time in half.

And the bristles! These days you've got your soft bristles, your medium bristles, your hard bristles, etc. Crest, I think, even has a brush now with uneven bristles, which has been "scientifically proven" to clean between teeth better. But think about that. How do they measure which toothbrush leaves more gunk between your teeth? And how do they collect it to measure it? And how do they find people willing to do the measuring?

Nothing is simple about toothbrushes these days.

The other day, for instance, I saw a commercial for the Aquafresh flex-neck toothbrush that "absorbs pressure to help protect gums." Which means what? That I've been subjecting my poor gums to too much pressure all these years? Why didn't someone tell me?

And then there are handles. I notice some brushes today have little strips of rough stuff on the handle, apparently so you won't slip and ram your toothbrush up your nose. Now, personally, this is not something I have ever done. But I figure the toothbrush company must know something – I mean, maybe they keep statistics on that sort of thing – so I may have to buy one.

That's the thing, isn't it? You never know which advance in toothbrush technology is the one you shouldn't ignore, so you buy them all.

That's what I do, anyway.

But you know what? I miss simplicity. I miss the days when there weren't so many choices. You wanted cereal? You had a choice between Rice Krispies or corn flakes. You want a car? Ford or GM. Take your pick.

Choices are killing us. We'd all be better off if we had fewer of them. Fewer brands of bread, fewer soda pops, fewer deodorants. And, really, couldn't we get along with just one type of toothbrush?

Of course we could.

As long as it has an angled head.

I like angled heads.

— December 14, 1992

Dish soap goes bad? The mind reels

You can't be too careful these days. Danger is everywhere. In the shadows near your ATM machine. In your wife's question about how her hair looks.

In the dish soap.

Yes, dish soap. Read your labels, people. You must learn to protect yourselves. I can't always be there for you.

My wife came home the other day with Dial dish-washing detergent. It was a departure from our regular brand, so I noticed straight away. We lead exciting lives.

This Dial, though, it's quite the product. Not only does it clean your dishes, but it contains an antibacterial hand cleanser and is citrus-scented to boot. Clean dishes, bacteria-free hands, plus the cool, refreshing scent of orange blossoms. Who could ask for more?

Marcia was enjoying some when she said, "What's this?"

I said, "What's what?"

"The dish soap, it has an expiration date."

The mind reels. Why would a dish soap need an expiration date? I can think of many things that need expiration dates.

Airplane engine mounts, for instance. Who knows how long those suckers have been hanging there on the wing like that?

Or kiwi fruit. You're supposed to buy them slightly gushy, but how do you know when gushy is too gushy?

Surgeons. If someone's going to cut on me, I want to know

if she's past her prime.

Neckties. A man pulls one of those really skinny ties out of the closet, notices it expired in 1981 and puts it back. "Whew," says the man. "That was close." A fashion *faux pas* avoided.

Pets. If pets had expiration dates, you'd avoid running out. "Honey, the cat's about to expire. Can you pick up another at the market?"

Relationships. With expiration dates, you'd know where you stand. "I can see by your expiration date that I'm due to be sick of you by tomorrow. Farewell forever, Clarisse."

I can also think of products that have expiration dates that don't need them. Soda pop, for instance. Pepsi made a big deal a few months ago about using "freshness labels."

Pop goes bad? If they hadn't told us, would we have noticed? Think about that. When's the last time you cracked open a Pepsi and said, "Bleah, stale"?

Never. You probably assumed pop was like Twinkies and Dick Clark – stuff that just doesn't grow old.

Dish soap's like that. What could go wrong with dish soap? But there it was on the label, in white and burgundy: Exp. 10/95. Of course, this should present no problem for us. We almost certainly will use up the soap before October. Hey. We're clean. But what if we don't? What would happen?

"Maybe it turns rancid," Marcia mused. "It's got citrus in it. Maybe that goes bad. Or maybe it means the chemicals break down and turn into something else, something horrible."

I couldn't say. This is what I get for not listening in science class. Just to be safe, I called the 800 number on the bottle and Marcy answered on the first ring. Things must not be hopping at Dial. I told her my wife had to know if her hands were going to disintegrate if she used old soap.

"Let me check the computer," she said.

When she came back, she said the computer said no, the soap doesn't go bad. "Some of the ingredients just aren't as effective after that date," she said.

Was I relieved! But why, I asked her, hadn't Dial told us about this potential problem before?

"I don't know," she said. "I think it's just something they do to sell the product."

Noooooooo.

— January 15, 1995

Stop and smell roses, apples, mint, oatmeal

We are afraid to smell like ourselves. That is why we try so hard to smell like something else.

These amazing thoughts hit me in the shower, as most of my amazing thoughts do.

I like showers. They are hot and soothing. Plus, you can count on a shower. There is a comforting routine to taking one.

Apple essence shampoo is not a part of my routine. But that's the name that was on the bottle of shampoo I held in my hand.

Standing there in the steam, I cursed my wife. (The shower is a good place to curse one's wife, as long as she is not in there with you.)

What had she done with my Ivory shampoo? I like my Ivory. It's white, bland, boring and nonsmelly.

This shampoo was green. Bright green. About the same shade of green as a green Lifesaver. I hate green Lifesavers. I give them away.

I sniffed it. It smelled like a green Lifesaver, too. I washed my hair with it anyway. There wasn't much choice. Afterward, I called my wife on the carpet.

"What did you do with my shampoo?" I demanded.

"We ran out," she replied. "I bought a new one. It was on sale. Do you like it?"

"No, I don't like it," I said. "What kind of a nut wants to

walk around smelling like a piece of fruit?"

"This nut," she said. Her voice had its hands on its hips. "And you'd better get used to it because we're not getting anything else until that bottle is gone."

It is a very big bottle.

And look what's in it: water, ammonium lauryl sulfate, ammonium laureth sulfate, lauramide DEA, citric acid, hydrooxypropyl, methylcellulose tetrasodium ETA, ammonium chloride, benzophenone-4, methylchloroisothiazalinone, methylisothizolinone, DMDM hydantoin ammonium, xylenesulfonate, FD&C blue No. 1, FD&C yellow No. 5.

But no apples. Better smell through chemistry. How quaint.

Why do we put stuff like this on our bodies? And why do we try so hard not to smell like ourselves? (Warning: Do not try this kind of deep thinking at home; columnists are trained professionals.)

I began to notice all the things I use to smell better each morning.

There's the shampoo. Then there's the conditioner, which smells vaguely like flowers. Then there's the soap, which, in our shower, is currently made out of oatmeal. It's good soap. It smells like oatmeal, too. And if you get hungry in there, you can eat it.

Then there's the liquid hand soap on the sink. It's orange and smells, I have decided, like methylisolimbergercheeseinone.

There is my shaving cream, which comes in an aluminum can and professes to smell like "cool menthol," as if cool smelled.

Then there is my deodorant. This month it's "surf spray." I have been to the ocean; it did not smell like "surf spray."

There is the aftershave that I use, coincidentally enough, after shaving. It's light green and has a smell that is ... nice. I'd give you a better description but that's all I keep coming up with. Nice. (Again, don't try this at home.)

Then there is the toothpaste, which smells minty. I'd never noticed it before, but my toothpaste is also freshness dated. "Do not use after date on bottom of tube," it warns, although I'm not too scared because it doesn't turn stale until July '97.

And finally there is the mouthwash, which tastes like the toothpaste, only mintier!

So after my daily clean-up, I smell like flowers, oatmeal, methylisorottingmeatinone, cool menthol, surf spray, green stuff and mint. That's a lot of smells. What am I covering up? I thought. Do I really smell that bad?

I decided to find out. My scheme was simple. I would not use any product that left an odor on me.

I showered without soap, brushed my teeth with baking soda and left my armpits unadorned. Then I carefully observed people's reaction to me to see if they acted as if I had stepped in a bog.

They didn't. No one asked me to step downwind. Nobody's tie curled when I spoke to them. Dogs did not run howling, house plants did not wilt. In fact, no one noticed except for my wife.

Phew, she said. You stink. Did you use deodorant? I explained my experiment. She just frowned and told me to knock it off.

Women. They simply don't understand science.

— September 28, 1994

Follow the Bouncing Ball

10 tips to help first-timers run right

It's Crim Road Race time again, and many of you are no doubt thinking, "Hey, I bet I could do that."

I understand this feeling. In fact, I was once a competitive runner: cross country, 2 mile, 5K, 10K, Special K. I ran them all.

After all, the urge to compete, to test one's mettle against one's peers, is a natural one. But then again, it's natural for lemmings to hurl themselves off cliffs, too.

So these days I cleave to the teachings of that great exercise philosopher, my wife, Marcia, who says, and I quote: "Marcias don't sweat. Not for anybody, not for anything."

It's not Plato, but it works for me, and I suggest you make it work for you, too.

But if not, if you are still foolishly thinking you might like to join the sweating herds that run the Crim, I have created the following 10-point guide to help you along.

1. Choose the proper attire – By this I do not mean that you should wear a tuxedo, although if you decide to do so you're in luck because I understand the course runs right by the mental health center.

What I do mean is that these days you can no longer run in a floppy T-shirt and ripped shorts. Spectators will laugh at you. You must wear silly neon short-shorts and a matching neon tank top that: 1) cost more than your car, and 2) were manufactured in total darkness by foreigners wearing safety goggles to shield their eyes from the harmful neon rays.

Of course, some runners opt for silly skin-tight lycra shorts. I do not recommend these, particularly if you are more than 5 ounces overweight, since from behind it will look like rival gangs of Jell-O are waging a violent turf war in your shorts.

2. Choose the right shoes – Your friendly neighborhood lending institution is standing by to help you with this one. Because these days, you cannot run in a pair of old canvas Converse shoes. Spectators would throw Gatorade at you. While it's still in the bottle. (Remember, this *is* Flint.)

No, you must wear costly air-filled running shoes such as the Reebok Pump, which, again, I do not recommend for the Crim since you will have to carry patches and an air pump in the event that you suffer a blowout.

3. Avoid sex the night before the race – Scientists recommend this, but then they're probably still bitter about not getting any dates back in high school, so I wouldn't pay too much attention.

4. The starting line – This is a good place to start. If you see throngs of people milling about restlessly shaking their legs, you have found the starting line. Either that or the line for the bathroom.

If it's the starting line, do not attempt to get anywhere near the front. Trust me on this one. And if you do, do not bend over to tie your shoe, because the moment you do the race will begin and you will die.

5. Follow the blue line – The Crim people have painted a blue line on the street this year for you to follow. This is because last year – and this is the truth – the pace car, driven by a Flint policeman, made a wrong turn and led runners astray. They still haven't been found.

By the way, there's no truth to the rumor that the mayor wanted the line drawn through AutoWorld to increase attendance.

6. Avoid international incidents – The Crim attracts runners from around the world. To be on the safe side, do not run between the Kuwaiti and the Iraqi runners.

7. Know your color codes – Runners must look out for one another, which is why the international runners' color-watch system was invented. For instance, if you are turning red,

other runners will know that you are exhausted, though not mortally so, and that they should simply step around your prone body.

Yellow means, "I have jaundice and should not be running in the first place."

Green means, "I am close to death. Notify my next of kin and cancel my magazine subscriptions."

Blue means, "Forget it, you're too late."

8. Do not eat a Super-Coney Deluxe with extra chili from Angelo's just prior to the race – Think of yourself. Think of your family. For god's sake, think of your fellow runners.

9. Control your emotions – If you are jogging along and a spectator suddenly throws a cup of water on you, do not grab him by the collar and say, "Why you little ..." He is trying to help. Or he simply likes throwing water on strangers. It's a tough call.

10. The finish line – This is a good place to end. If you see throngs of people collapsed in the arms of other people gasping "Never again, never ever again" between violent bouts of retching, you have found the finish line.

Congratulations! You've finished your first Crim.

Now go home.

Your color's terrible.

— August 23, 1990

Bouncing between myth and real men

AUBURN HILLS – To my left, center William Bedford sat naked on a stool, picking at his long toes.

Behind me, in a little room, Dennis Rodman mutely rode an exercise bike, elastic ice packs strapped to both knees.

To my right, John Salley was talking trash to anything catching his eye: the ball boy, forward David Greenwood, the wall, his hairbrush. "Hey, yo," he'd yell. "Hey, yo ..."

It was a few days before the New Year and my cherished Detroit Pistons had just defeated the New Jersey Nets. In the tiny locker room of The Palace, a gaggle of reporters waited for Isiah, Vinnie and the rest of the team to come out of the showers.

I waited with them, not as a reporter, but as a fan whose influential father-in-law had arranged a special pass, a pass most sports fans would kill for, a pass that only made me think, "Geez, I gotta get out of here."

And so I did, whipping out the door and into the labyrinth of tunnels beneath the stands, a feeling of relief washing over me like a cool wave.

Since then I've thought a lot about why I did that.

Certainly a part of me was embarrassed to be breathlessly awaiting the arrival of a bunch of naked men. I've never understood how sports writers can do that. Maybe they get used to it.

And, no doubt, I felt a bit like a groupie, being there, as I was, for no official purpose. I've never understood groupies either. Maybe they don't understand themselves.

But I think the main reason I didn't stay is I didn't want anything to ruin my fantasy.

See, I've always loved sports, the romance and mystery of it all.

I remember as a kid reading and rereading a biography of Bart Starr, the quarterback for the Green Bay Packers during their Titletown glory years.

The book was one of those starry-eyed things for youngsters, filled with tales of Bart's virtuous struggle; how he'd thrown pass after pass through an old tire until, one day, he'd won a zillion championships.

It said nothing about whether Bart, as a youngster, pulled the wings off flies. Or whether Bart, as an adult, beat his dog, ignored his wife or spat on reporters. Even if he had, that wasn't the point.

Fantasy was, and that's still how I like my sports.

I don't care about the business of sports, about contracts and salary caps and labor strikes. Tell me about balls and strikes.

I don't want to know that Joe Glitz takes steroids or that he's a drunk. I don't want to know that he charges little kids for his autograph. I don't want to know that he's a gambling, carousing jerk.

What I want to know about are the touchdowns and slam dunks, about the home runs and the Hail Marys. I want to know about strength and courage, about rising to the challenge and succeeding against all odds.

I want to know about men who throw footballs through tires.

I realize this is not a realistic attitude. Athletes, after all, are people, too. They have problems and flaws. But, near as I can tell, reality has very little to do with sports, fantasy everything.

Why else would we spend so much time watching full-grown adults play children's games for millions of dollars? Why else would we endure the spitting, the grabbing and the butt patting? They don't pat butts in the real world do they? They certainly don't at my office.

The psychologists will tell you we watch sports out of a need to belong to something larger than ourselves. And maybe that's part of it. But I watch to be transported into another world, where deadlines and pressures don't exist, where the child in me can imagine being out there breaking tackles or sliding home.

It's a fragile illusion, one that's not easy to maintain in adulthood. Illusions rarely are.

My wife, for instance, has always loved the music of Cat Stevens. He's the guy who sang "Peace Train," "Moon Shadow" and other songs of peace and harmony back in the '70s.

He's also the Muslim who declared a few months ago that he'd happily kill Salman Rushdie, author of "The Satanic Verses," if he had the chance.

My wife hasn't played his music since. For her, the bubble has been popped, the illusion shattered. Knowledge is often fatal to fantasy.

This crossed my mind as I stood in the Pistons locker room. I didn't want to meet the men, I realized. I wanted to meet the myths. Maybe, in this case, they were one and the same, but maybe not.

And so I left.

Why take chances, right?

— January 15, 1990

To tolerate softball, play by these rules

Millions of women enjoy playing softball. Dozens more enjoy watching their husbands play softball.

And then there is my wife.

To say that Marcia has simply a mild disinterest in the game is to say that Bill Clinton has merely a slight affection for cheeseburgers.

She is profound in her disinterest. If you gave her a choice between watching a softball game and having her head shaved by blind monkeys, she would think about it.

Why this is, I don't know.

Personally, I can't think of anything more enjoyable than sitting in the hot sun watching sweaty men with beer bellies and bad attitudes scuffle around in the dirt after a ball.

But you know women.

Now, understand, this doesn't mean that Marcia doesn't go to my games.

Because she does, and she does so for three reasons.

1. I love playing softball.
2. She loves me.
3. I threaten to never again pick my underwear up off the floor if she doesn't attend.

You may ask, "But if she doesn't want to go, why do you make her go?"

And the answer is: Because I'm a husband. That's what husbands do.

I'm surprised I have to tell you that.

Anyway, suffice it to say she has been to a LOT of games. So many, in fact, that she has decided to share with the rest of the world her expertise in this area.

And, thus, we present "Marcia's Guide to Surviving Your Significant Other's Softball Game, Assuming You Can't Whine Enough to Get Out of Going Altogether".

1. Bring the proper equipment. Sitting on the bleachers is for amateurs and people who don't mind sore butts. Standard equipment includes a comfortable folding chair, a Walkman, lemonade and a good book.

2. Also bring sunglasses. Not only will they protect your eyes, but no one will be able to tell if you nod off.

3. Sit with other softball wives and girlfriends. This will give you someone with whom you can trade softball complaints, which any veteran game-goer will tell you is the key to a good time. If you're a rookie and can't come up with any good complaints on your own, a fairly popular one is, "Can you believe it, they act just like little kids out there."

4. Cheer. It doesn't matter when. Just cheer for a few seconds every five minutes or so. He'll think you're interested, then you can go back to your book or whatever.

5. Don't ask, "Why do you spit like that?" or "Does that guy at shortstop have some sort of fungal problem or something? He keeps adjusting himself."

Remember: No one really knows why ballplayers scratch, spit and adjust themselves so often. They just do, that's all.

6. When sitting with other women, appoint a designated watcher. This idea is based on the designated driver concept. One person watches the game and takes notes while the rest chat, read or scope for cute butts.

After the game, the designated watcher gives each of the nonwatchers a detailed report on how her husband and/or boyfriend did.

This allows each woman to know what the heck her respective male is talking about when he asks (and he will): "Did you see me A) slide into home B) single to left or C) trip over my feet on the way to third?"

7. Do not drink liquids! I can't emphasize this enough. Liquid intake equals trips to the Port-a-John, which are to be avoided at all costs.

8. If you want to embarrass the hell out of your husband, walk over behind the team bench and ask him, in a motherly tone that everyone can hear, "You look tired. Are you all right?" He won't invite you to a game for a month.

9. If all else fails, remember these two important words: No-Doz.

10. Milk it for all it's worth. You go to his games, he goes to the mall with you. On a Saturday. You go to a double-header. He cleans out the garage AND goes to the mall with you. Don't let him weasel out of this. Remember, he owes you. Big time.

— July 12, 1993

Baseball catches you and holds on

Baseball is a funny game. It grabs a boy, shakes him up until the dreams start to rise in him like bubbles in a Coke, then it spits him out.

"Not good enough."

Most of us hear the words sooner or later. I heard them sooner. All glove, no hit. That was my label. And unfortunately it was an accurate one.

The highest I got was Babe Ruth baseball, where I never even made the all-star team. Although my brother, the coach, swears I almost did.

"The other second basemen could hit just a little better," he said. "You understand."

I said I did, but I lied.

When it comes to baseball and boys, dreams die hard, if ever.

I'm not bitter. I was then, but not now. Honest. At 31, I still love baseball. I follow the bigs religiously. I'm in a fantasy league, and I live for the morning box scores. Rotball geek, that's me.

And I'm still pretty good at softball. Not as good as I used to be when I was younger and filled with the anger of trying to prove what I hadn't proved before – that I was a ballplayer, that I belonged, that I could do it.

But I still enjoy it. I still remind myself – jokingly now – not to go swimming prior to a game, which was my Little League coach's mysterious weekly admonishment.

I still get that tiny tingle of excitement in my stomach before a game.

The little second baseman in me still wants to go for an A&W root beer after the game. (I settle for real beer now. *C'est la vie.*)

And yet part of me knows that softball isn't the same. Part of me realizes it's a poor man's version of baseball, a game played on a smaller field with a bigger ball by aging adolescents with rickety arms, swollen midriffs and a marked aversion to sliding (strawberries and dress slacks not mixing).

Softball is Baseball Lite and a cruel reminder to its participants that they are not what they used to be.

Most of us, in our heart of hearts, know this. We simply choose to ignore it. As I said, baseball dreams die hard.

Which is why, every now and then, a guy finds himself at a batting cage. He doesn't even mean to pull into the place. He's just driving around, killing time, when he sees the cages and decides to watch.

The cages, even on this chilly, cloudy day, are full of dreamers: kids wearing wobbly batting helmets looking to the future; adults wearing spare tires longing for the past.

And suddenly, before he knows it, he is joining them. He is digging into his pocket and heading for the "medium" cage to find out if he still has what he never had to begin with.

A batting cage is a time machine. Clearly. The sign doesn't say so, but it is. You see the fat guy in the next cage? The one corkscrewing himself into the paddock with each miss? Inside, at this moment, he is 12, wearing a baggy, ill-fitting uniform, and he is the best, most fiercest hitter in the league.

The father outside the medium cage? The one carping at his son to concentrate, stride into the pitch, stop pulling the ball, go to right, keep your head on the ball, c'mon, you can do better ...?

That's not his son in there.

That's him.

And you. Each pitch takes you further back. With each miss, you relive past failures, little indignities, small horrors. Remember that time you made three errors in one inning?

Whiff!

Remember the time you tripped over your own stirrups as

you rounded third and were tagged out?

Whiff!

Remember riding the pines? Remember ... tryouts?!

Whiff! Whiff!

In batting cages, as in life, there seem to be two whiffs for every solid whack. But, oh, those whacks.

When you hit a baseball well, when the ball spits off the bat like a watermelon seed, there's no better feeling in the world. None. Ask any guy who ever dreamed about being a ballplayer when he grew up.

WHACK! ZOOOM!

It is for that feeling that batting cages exist. You enter them, you enter another world. You enter ... your past.

Baseball is indeed a funny game. It grabs a boy and never lets go, even when the boy grows up and he knows beyond certainty that the fizz in his Coke has long since fizzled out.

— May 16, 1993

Here's why hoops reign over hockey

It's basketball season once again.

My time of year.

I love hoops. I play it. I watch it. I follow it. In my book, it's right up there with baseball, which is saying a lot, since baseball, I am firmly convinced, is the Lord's game. (He was a crackerjack shortstop in his youth.)

A buddy disagrees.

He says baseball and basketball are boring games whose limited appeal has been all but destroyed by high salaries and monster egos.

His game is hockey. He thinks it's a great game. As proof, he showed me a column by a Detroit writer who came up with a list earlier this month of 21 reasons why hockey is better than hoops.

This list, I feel, deserves a response. Here, then, are 22 reasons hockey doesn't light my fire and basketball does:

1. An exciting hockey game is 0-0. A really exciting hockey game is 1-0. And a real barn-burner is a 2-1.

2. In basketball, there's a lot of scoring. A 2-1 score in basketball is a fairly tame three seconds.

3. You need binoculars to see the puck in hockey. Get beyond the third row and, if you can see it at all, it looks like a raisin. And I've always been against fruit abuse.

4. Hockey is bad boxing on skates. If they want to fight that badly, they ought to try the welterweight division.

5. In basketball, there is the three-point shot, which is one of the most exciting plays in sports, next to Morganna the Kissing Bandit wobbling onto the court or field after an athlete. Hockey would be a lot more exciting with a three-point play. It would also be more exciting with Morganna, come to think of it.

6. Basketball also has the slam dunk, which is one of the most exciting plays in sports next to a crash at Indy, many of which are caused, incidentally, when a driver catches a glimpse of Morganna.

7. When a hockey player gets mad at you, he pulls your jersey up over your head so you can't fight back, which is a pretty wussy thing to do if you ask me.

8. Hockey has the blue line. I don't understand what a blue line is. I know a group of players a team puts together on the ice is called a line. So is a blue line a bunch of guys who are seriously depressed?

9. I can't skate. I do, however, have a mean turn-around.

10. It's cold at a hockey game. I don't like any sporting event at which my nose runs.

11. I have yet to see someone's bare butt at a basketball game. I went to a hockey game once where the fans in front of us wore their trousers so low that they mooned us each time they sat down, which, thank God, wasn't often. I am told this is a common occurrence at hockey games. Maybe they should post signs. "Remember: Crack kills."

12. Bill Laimbeer, who is so mean he can get away with running like a girl without anyone teasing him about it.

13. Hockey players wear baggy uniforms. Being the fashion plate that I am, I find this terribly distasteful.

14. They allow tie games in hockey. That's not only boring, it's downright un-American.

15. Hockey reminds me of painful childhood memories. I couldn't play hockey then because I had weak ankles. I once tried playing one of those table-top hockey games where you have to twist and shove the knobs, but I wasn't very good at that, either. Even my wrists had weak ankles.

16. You go to a hockey game, you can get hit with a puck and die. The most that can happen to you at a basketball game is that Charles Barkley will spit at you.

17. Players can enter a hockey game whenever they feel like

it, which is pretty disorderly if you ask me.

18. No one throws an octopus onto the playing surface at a basketball game the way they do at hockey games. The only thing they throw at basketball games is elbows.

19. Slamming into someone in hockey is called "checking." What is NOT slamming into them called? Savings? (Rim shot.)

20. In basketball, everyone wants to be like Michael Jordan. In hockey, they all want to be the Hanson brothers from the movie "Slapshot," who were uglier than the south end of a northbound mule.

21. There are no cheerleaders in hockey. If there were, they'd have to wear fur coats and mukluks.

22. Everybody makes the playoffs in hockey. They play 9 zillion games to eliminate two teams. What's the point of that?

Case closed.

— October 26, 1992

Putting the UM loss behind us

Dear Michigan State fans: Hi! It's your old pals, the long-suffering fans of the University of Michigan Wolverines.

We know, we know. You think we're bitter, right? To which we say: That hurts. That really, really hurts. We thought you knew us better than that. Bitter? Us? Pshaw!

I mean, hey, we're glad your team won the big game last Saturday. In fact, that's why we're writing: We want to congratulate you on a contest well-played. Way to go, guys! You deserved to win! And we mean that! Cross our little maize-and-blue hearts!

(Did you see that idiotic call at the end of the game?!!!)

Oh, we know. You expected us to rant and rave and throw a classic Schembechler-esque fit about those idiot referees who 1) didn't flag the FLAGRANT pass interference by YOUR defender on OUR receiver during that 2-point conversion attempt that would have won US the game, and 2) then said OUR guy didn't catch the ball.

(Which he did.)

You probably expected us to cry about how we wuz robbed and how we coulda been a contendah and all that.

Maybe you even expected us to do something outrageous, like write you a Trojan Horse letter. You know, on the surface all nicey-nice, while hidden between the lines are subliminal messages – secretly encoded by top-level UM scientists – that only your subconscious can perceive.

Ha ha! How silly! As if the technology existed for such a thing! Hoo, you Spartans sure have active imaginations!

(Wake up and smell the coffee! Your guy was hanging on our guy like a cheap suit!!! Anyone could see that!)

So, anyway, maybe in the past we would have done those rotten, nasty, infantile things after losing a big game. *(Which was rightfully ours.)* But that was the old us. We've changed. We're kinder, gentler, thousand-points-of-light kinda fans now. Wolverine Fans Lite. Yeah. That's us.

(Listen to us carefully: You are getting veeerry sleepy ...)

Of course, you could hardly blame us if we did overreact. You have to admit, it's not like UM has ever caught a break from the zebras. You remember the 1979 Rose Bowl, where USC's Charles White scored the infamous "phantom touchdown" that cost us the game? Or how about last year's Rose Bowl: Remember that asinine holding penalty on our fake punt? We ground our teeth so much after that one that we woke up the next day with a mouthful of dust.

(You are now in our power. You will petition the Big Ten to review the game film ...)

We used to think that maybe the refs had an axe to grind with Bo. But now that Gary Moeller's the head coach, we figure it's gotta be that they've got something against the entire *university!* Like maybe they applied to UM when they were students and didn't get in. Something like that.

(And if they somehow fail to overturn the call and give the game to Michigan, we want you to ...)

Not that we're upset, mind you. That complaining stuff, it's all behind us. Refs are human, too. They make mistakes.

(... forfeit the game to us ...)

Hey, we realize that it's just a game, just good clean fun. Certainly not life or death or anything. Ha. Ha ha!

(And while you're at it, drop and give us 20. And call us "sir.")

So, again, congrats! And don't worry about us, we'll be fine.

(When we snap our fingers, you will awaken and remember nothing but this: George Perles wears women's underwear.)

Sincerely: Your pals at UM.

— October 18, 1990

Dancing for the gold OK by me

Far be it from me to make fun of the International Olympic Committee for making ballroom dancing a provisional sport.

They already have ice dancing, don't they? Of course they do. My wife makes me watch it.

So why not ballroom dancing?

I'll admit, it's odd knowing I could someday flip on ESPN and see little Freddie Nebbish, the kid in my neighborhood with the post nasal drip and the mom who made him take ballroom dancing lessons, being interviewed after winning a gold medal: "I (sniff) would like to (sniff, blow, wipe) thank my coach Maurice and of course (snorrrrrk!) my mother for making this possible. HONNNNNNNK!"

Still, ballroom dancing is certainly no dumber than other Olympic sports. Synchronized swimming, for instance. This is not a sport. This is simulated drowning. I watch synchronized swimming and I have this overwhelming urge to toss a Baby Ruth bar in the pool. (If you've seen the classic motion picture "Caddyshack" you know what I'm talking about.)

The bobsled? Gravity is not a sport. And who is this Bob character, anyway?

Fencing? They like to puff up fencing by using fancy-schmancy terms like foil, parry and thrust, but when you boil it down it's still just pretend sword fighting.

Curling? My wife's hairdresser was, like, totally crushed

when he found out this event had nothing to do with blow-dryers and styling gel.

Bowling? This was once an Olympic demonstration sport. But they ruined it by eliminating the Beer Frame.

Ski jumping? This does not take skill. This takes an IQ of 12. And gravity. Gravity is not a sport.

Cross-country skiing? I'd rather watch grass grow. Hell, I'd rather mow grass.

The best part about ballroom dancing in the Olympics is that America is bound to do well. Think about it: In how many other countries is ballroom dancing popular? For that matter, how many other countries have ballrooms or even know what one is?

I think ballroom dancing is a sign the Olympics are becoming Americanized, and I say it's about time. Most Olympic sports have their roots in other nations, other cultures, and American athletes have had to learn their games. (Need I mention, ick, soccer?)

Let the world play our games for a change. Let's also see:

- Softball. Losing team buys the beer.
- Euchre. Husband-and-wife teams, like real life. Your husband trumps your ace, you rip out his lungs.
- Monster trucking. First one to crush 10 rusty Chevys wins.
- All-Star Wrestling. It is NOT fake.
- Deer hunting. Points for biggest rack, longest shot, biggest hangover and the biggest lie about all of the above.
- Country line dancing. There's no athletic skill involved, unless you count the ability to hook your thumbs in your belt, but it would really tick off the French, who hate American stuff like this.
- Two-person modern dance. An American classic. Woman asks man to dance. Man mutters that he looks like a turkey in heat when he dances. Woman says, oh, c'mon. Man relents. Woman proceeds to dance with wild, rhythmic abandon, like a tornado unleashed. Man proceeds to dance arhythmically, like he's having a seizure, thereby alerting amorous turkeys for miles around.

This would be my event. I would rule.

If you're nice to me, I'll let you touch my medal.

— May 8, 1995

U.P. Living

Yooper offers winter wisdom to down under

Pardon my frankness, but some of you people down here can be such snow wimps.

Honestly. We get a little snow – a mere 6 inches! – and folks panic. Schools and businesses close. Drivers fling themselves into ditches. People start laying in supplies, just in case.

It's amazing. Up in the Upper Peninsula, the land from whence I proudly hail, that little bit of precipitation we had Tuesday would be considered a flurry, just God with a mild case of dandruff scratching Her head.

This isn't winter. Winter is what we had back when I was a kid and we had to snowshoe 40 miles a day to school through drifts 12 feet high. And it was so cold your spit froze before it hit the ground.

(That's nothing. In my daddy's day, or so he tells it, the distance to the same school was 80 miles, the drifts were 24 feet high, and it was so cold your lips froze shut so you couldn't spit. But then it's a well-known meteorological fact that a father's boyhood winters are always twice as bad as his son's.)

Down here you don't even have winter. You have long, wet, gray falls. It's depressing. You get snow, but it doesn't stay long. I bought cross-country skis two winters ago; I've been able to use them twice.

That's what gets me. You've got all the drawbacks of winter

– cold, slush, bad roads, the Bob Hope Christmas special – and none of the benefits: pine trees bent low with snow; glistening vistas of unbroken powder; towering snow forts built by apple-cheeked children; icicles long enough to use as swords.

And snowmen. I miss real snowmen. Snowmen the size of Raymond Burr. Here there's usually only enough snow for a snowman the size of Dudley Moore.

It's no wonder some of you freak when a real blow hits. You're not used to this stuff, which is why I have come up with the following guide to surviving winter U.P.-style:

1. Language – If you want to handle winter like a Yooper, you must learn to speak like us. Just as Eskimos have 40 different words for snow, we Yoopers have dozens of colorful phrases to describe the various aspects of winter.

For example, whereas a Loper (a Lower Peninsula resident, aka "Troll" or "Mittenhead") might describe a particularly chilly day as "a particularly chilly day," a Yooper would describe it as "colder'na witch's kiss." (I'm cleaning that up for print, but you get the idea.)

Or take Tuesday's snow. A Loper might exclaim, "My, what deep snow!" Whereas a Yooper would say, "It's deeper'na a polar bear's butt ootdare."

Adding "Eh?" "ya know" or "you betcha" to the end of each phrase is optional, but highly recommended.

2. Canceling school – They cancel school for anything down here: an inch of snow, a faulty furnace, a really stiff breeze. Get real. School should only be canceled if the school superintendent looks out his window and can't look out his window.

3. Snowplows – I am writing this on Tuesday afternoon. If I go home tonight and my street is plowed, I will be amazed. If it is plowed by next Tuesday I will be amazed.

What is there in this town, one snowplow? What we need is a vast, gleaming fleet of monster plows, like we had in the U.P., the kind of big, ripsnorting rumblehunks I used to have nightmares about. We could also use some genuine, wild-eyed U.P. snowplow jockeys, the type who will bury your car under a slushy 12-foot mound if you forget and leave it parked on the street.

4. Dress – I see you guys walking around with those rubber

footie things slipped daintily over your dress shoes. I see you ladies clutching the collar of your thin, meager overcoats and taking those comical, mincing steps on the ice in your high heel shoes. Where do you think you are, California?

This is Michigan. What you need is a good, solid, traditional U.P. unisex winter wardrobe: flannel shirts, Sears long johns, a Green Bay Packers stocking cap or "chook," a snowmobile suit, preferably with "Polaris" or "Ski-doo" on the back, and a pair of Red Wing boots.

You'll know you're properly dressed if people can't tell whether you would use the "Bucks" or the "Does" restroom at the bar.

5. Food – "Stokin da furnace" is important, especially if you're going ice fishing. Wilford Brimley is right – oatmeal is the right thing to do, although not necessarily a tasty way to do it. Add some fresh maple syrup. I know a nice tree.

Also, for when those big storms hit, it's a good idea to lay in a stock of potatoes and "rutabagers" (the U.P. version of rutabagas) for making pasties (pronounced "pass-teez" not "pay-steez").

These items are best kept in your root cellar where they won't freeze. If you don't have a root cellar, dig one, unless you live in an apartment, in which case the downstairs neighbors might complain.

6. Shovels – I went out shopping for a shovel the other night and I couldn't believe my eyes. There on the racks were plastic shovels. Plastic! For dealing with ice and snow and sludge! Forget the plastic. Steel shovels are the way to go. Steel push shovels are OK, but a steel coal shovel is best.

7. Driving – Some so-called "experts" might tell you that the secret to winter driving is going real slow and pumping your brakes when you need to stop. And maybe in Florida, where they call out the National Guard at the sight of the first snowflake, this is true.

But any Yooper will tell you that if you drive slowly you can't break through the drifts or that ridge of snow the plow leaves in front of your driveway, plus brakes are for sissies, although they do come in handy while doing doughnuts in the Shopko parking lot. (And please don't tell me you don't know what doing doughnuts is.)

No. A true Yooper needs just three things for successful

winter driving:

1) A good set of tire chains.

2) Three 50-pound bags of salt or feed to sling in the back for traction.

3) A pickup truck, preferably a rusted Chevy with Hank Williams Jr. on the eight track.

So there you have it. I hope these tips help you become less of a snow sissy.

As for me, I've got to get home.

God just scratched Her head again, and that driveway ain't going to shovel itself, ya know?

— January 16, 1992

Yooper tips for da cold weather

A few years ago, as a public service, I offered you tips on how to deal with heavy winter snows Yooper-style.

My main qualification for doing so is that I was raised in the Upper Peninsula and therefore have some experience with snow so deep you have to use a snorkel.

Anyway, now that we here in Michigan's banana belt have suffered a nasty Arctic blast, I thought I would perform another public service by revealing, for the first time, the secrets behind how Yoopers cope with the bitter cold.

1. First and foremost, stop your bellyaching. Yoopers don't complain about the cold because Yoopers have a keen sense of geography and therefore realize that this is Michigan and in Michigan, repeat after me, WINTER HAPPENS!

2. Wear plaid. Plaid is the warmest fabric known to man.

Now, you might be thinking, "Wait a minute, plaid isn't a fabric, it's a style of fabric."

OK, you've got me there. But there is something about plaid that is warmer than all other styles. It's true. Take two shirts made of the same material, one in plaid, the other in any other style. The plaid one will always feel warmer.

I don't know why this is, it just is. Scientists at The Plaid Research Institute & Gas 'N' Go in the booming U.P. metropolis of Ralph (population 28, although Ginnie Ingvaark is expecting twins any day now) are investigating this phenomenon as we speak. Their leading theory is that the intersecting lines in a plaid shirt somehow trap body heat. I'm serious. Why do you think so many Yoopers wear plaid? It can't be the bold fashion statement alone.

3. Don't watch the weather report. This is a leading cause of depression about the cold, not to mention bricks thrown through TV screens. Yoopers ignore weather reports for the simple reason that there are only two seasons north of the bridge: summer and the other 351 days of the year.

4. Get yourself a subscription to Playboy. That'll warm you up in a hurry. If you're a guy, I mean. (Or, I suppose, if you're Newt Gingrich's sister.) Ladies, for you I suggest a subscription to Playgirl, a copy of the latest Brad Pitt movie or a virgin credit card.

5. Consume mass quantities of the official U.P. winter beverage, which is Stroh's, Blatz or Miller High Life, depending on what costs the least down to the Red Owl. You may call it imbibing. In the U.P., we call it antifreeze.

6. Carry an ice pick with you when you head to the outhouse. There's nothing worse than being unprepared for a frozen hole. (Secret note to fellow Yoopers: I know no one uses outhouses in da U.P. anymore, but da trolls think we do and it amuses them, so what da heck.)

7. Punch out any wise guy who says "Cold? P'shaw, this ain't cold. Why, when I was a kid it got down to 400 below! And we didn't walk to school, we tunneled!"

8. Learn to play euchre. It's the official game of the Upper Peninsula and will take your mind off how cold it is. An interesting winter variation on this game is "backward strip euchre." Winner of each hand gets to put something on.

9. Hibernate. Bears do it. Yoopers do it. Why not you? Hop in bed, cover up and leave a wake-up call for May. It's the only sensible thing to do.

10. Above all else, do not go outside. Yoopers are keenly aware of the fact that – follow this closely – outside is where the cold is.

Remember: Cold weather is God's way of telling you to stay inside and watch "Wheel of Fortune."

— December 17, 1995

Gov. Clinton needs lesson in geography

I would hate to think that one off-the-cuff remark might cost Bill Clinton the election, but it could happen.

In discussing President Bush's Labor Day walk across the Mackinac Bridge, Clinton, who visits Michigan on Tuesday, had Bush "walking across the wonderful bridge that connects Mackinac Island to the mainland in Michigan."

For shame, governor. You blew it on two counts.

One, there is no bridge connecting Mackinac Island with Michigan or with anything else.

Two, the Lower Peninsula is not the "mainland." Saying so is enough to make any Yooper's blood boil.

In fact, we Yoopers tend to think of our own beautiful peninsula as the "main" land.

Look at the facts:

Geographically, the U.P. resembles a big, friendly hand stretching out from the great state of Wisconsin (motto: "Cows R Us") to pat the Lower Peninsula on the head as if to say, "There, there, Detroit's not so bad."

And what does the Lower Peninsula look like? A silly little mitten.

The U.P. has towering trees, pristine streams and wonderfully warm people. And the L.P. has, well, just plain old regular trees, streams and people.

The U.P. has lush, velvety snow in the winter. The L.P. has ... slush.

The U.P. has the Soo Locks, the Mackinac Bridge (yes, it's ours) and the world-famous Mystery Spot. The only locks in the L.P. are on the doors, the only bridge of note is the Zilwaukee Bridge, which is an international joke, and the only mystery spot is the spot where Jimmy Hoffa is buried.

I could go on and on.

The point, governor, is that you'd better hope the election isn't close because you've just lost the support of 245,000 Yoopers and countless expatriates like me, whose body is stuck in the L.P. but whose heart will forever and always remain plaid.

Your only hope of regaining our good graces and repairing the enormous potential damage to your candidacy is to eradicate your ignorance about the Great White North. And how can you do that?

Glad you asked.

You can take this handy-dandy quiz, which I have entitled, "Everything Ya Wanted Ta Know About Yoopers But Were Afraid Ta Ask."

1. The Upper Peninsula is:

A) An economically depressed region of the state of Michigan frequently ignored by state and federal government. (Hint, hint.)

B) A lot harder to form than the Lower Peninsula when making a map of Michigan with your hands.

C) The land of the free, home of the mosquito.

2. When we finally declare ourselves an independent state, it will be called:

A) Anything we damn well want to call it. You gotta problem with that?

B) Sure as hell not North Michigan.

C) Superior.

3. In this new state the state flag will be:

A) Flown from every bar.

B) Lowered to half staff whenever a great American like Little Jimmy Dickens or Hank Williams Jr. dies.

C) Plaid.

4. The state bird would be:

A) A dead pheasant.

B) A dead woodcock.

C) A dead partridge.

5. A pasty is:
   A) Deeeeelicious!
   B) Where rutabagas go to die.
   C) A Cornish meat and vegetable pie, and don't pronounce it "pay-stee," hear?
6. The beer of choice in the U.P. is:
   A) Stroh's.
   B) Miller.
   C) Red White and Blue, Altes, Buckhorn, Schlitz, Pabst, Budweiser, Rolling Rock, Weidman ...
7. A dead skunk in the middle of the road is:
   A) The name of a really funny song.
   B) Something to steer at.
   C) Dinner.
8. A "chook" is:
   A) A stocking cap.
   B) The same as a "took."
   C) The sound a frozen engine makes on a Yooper February morn.
9. The "Humongous Fungus" is:
   A) A giant mushroom discovered in the U.P., which is reported to be, next to Dom DeLuise, the world's largest living organism.
   B) What we call John Engler.
   C) What your uncle gets on his foot after standing in the creek for too long with leaky waders.
10. The most popular activity in the U.P. is:
   A) Shootin' or catchin' things.
   B) Stuffing things we shoot or catch.
   C) Lying about the size of the things we tried to shoot or catch.
11. The second most popular activity in the U.P. is:
   A) Going to Shopko, eh?
   B) Looking for work, eh?
   C) Taking stupid troll tourists out snipe hunting or cow-tipping, eh?
12. A Yooper's wardrobe (men) is not complete without:
   A) A snowmobile suit.
   B) Swampers.
   C) A Green Bay Packers chook.
13. A Yooper's wardrobe (women) is not complete without:

A) A snowmobile suit.
B) A flannel nightgown.
C) Fur-lined pantyhose.

14. The biggest industry in the U.P. is:
A) The party store industry.
B) The party store industry.
C) The party store industry (this is a toughie, eh?)

15. The proper way to end a sentence in the U.P. is to:
A) Say, "Eh?"
B) Say, "Ya know?"
C) Spit.

The answer to all of the above questions, Mr. Clinton, is D, all of the above, which wasn't one of the answers, true, but who ever said life was fair?

You have now been educated, governor.

Now go forth and profane no more, eh?

— *August 5, 1992*

Fear hops on for ride in the city

It was night and we were in a small grassy area next to the old cement grandstands in my old hometown, Escanaba, population: not a whole lot.

I leaned on a chain-link fence raptly watching my Eskymos whip the hated Gladstone Braves in their annual high school football game, which is the second biggest event of the year around these parts behind the opening of deer season.

Marcia sat Indian-style against the fence, cradling our 20-month-old son, who was fast asleep. (He has little use for football, as he realizes he is someday going to play for the Detroit Tigers.)

"Look," she said, nodding toward the patch of grass over my shoulder.

Believe me when I tell you there was nothing special going on. A few kids, no older than 5, were wrestling. A few slightly older kids giggled and chased one another. Some preteens practiced their awkward mating dances.

"So?" I said.

"So there aren't any parents around. Did you notice?"

I hadn't and there weren't. The parent in me instantly thought: My god, anybody could kidnap these kids! Anybody could sell them drugs! Why aren't they being supervised? Where are their parents?! How can they sit in the stands watching football when ...

Then I got it. There weren't any parents around because there was no need for parents to be around. Mom and Dad were up in the stands enjoying the game. And they knew without thinking that their kids were safe because Escanaba is a small town, and in small towns fear is a stranger.

I'd almost forgotten that. I've lived in big cities for the past 11 years.

In that time, I have acquired big-city habits. I lock my car door even if I'm running into a convenience store. I have an alarm system on my house. I keep a suspicious eye on strangers in my neighborhood.

In short, I have learned the language of the city, the language of fear. Or maybe it's merely doubt. Or worry. Yes, worry. You live in the city, you worry about what could happen because it has happened so many times before.

Understand. I am not trying to trash cities here. I love them, their energy. I live in one now by choice. But there is an undeniable cost to city living.

Innocence. You lose some innocence. When I was a youngster, I would hop on my banana bike and go everywhere and nowhere with my friends. On Saturdays we would leave our homes after breakfast and not return until dinner. Our mothers never worried because they didn't have to. What could happen to us?

Here in the city, parents I know don't allow their children of bicycling age to go more than a block from the house because they are afraid.

And with good reason. One kid I know had his bike taken from him by some young toughs in my neighborhood. Another watched pie-eyed a shooting in the park two blocks from my house.

What floors me, given the place I grew up, is how normal this all is for today's city kids. They don't taste the joy of freedom until well into their teen years, and even then there is always that voice in the background telling them: Be careful, beware, watch out.

I realize I am idealizing here. Small towns today often wear their big brothers' hand-me-downs. Drugs, crime, abuse. There are few Mayberrys left these days.

But it certainly is true that small towns have far less of the bad stuff that spins our wheels. Small towns, by their nature, seem to have retained a good deal of their innocence and magic.

So I've been thinking. It won't be long before my son is of the running-around age. Should I move back to small-town America for him? Doesn't he deserve the same chance at the relatively carefree childhood that I experienced? Or is that running away?

I have a feeling I know what the kid in me would say.

— October 30, 1995

I'm learning my hometown is not so bad

I was walking along Lake Michigan on a warm, cloudless morning in Escanaba, my hometown in the Upper Peninsula, when I came across the telescope.

It was in a park near downtown that I rarely visited in all the years I lived there, so I hadn't noticed it before. It was the type of telescope you see at the Grand Canyon. Drop in a quarter and you can look around for a few minutes. So that's what I did.

I looked northwest across Little Bay de Noc toward the bedroom town of Gladstone.

Then I swung the lens east toward the distant Stonington Peninsula, where they used to mine limestone.

Then I studied a lighthouse near the mouth of the harbor, then the great mounds of iron ore waiting at the docks for the big lake boats to lug south.

Finally, I stared out at the vast, dark lake herself – my cherished Michigan, queen of them all.

Beautiful, I thought. What a nice place I grew up in.

That simple thought startled me.

I hadn't felt that way about Escanaba for years.

In fact, I'm ashamed to admit that I hated the place when I left 15 years ago and wasn't too fond of it in many of the years since.

The reasons hardly matter now: perceived slights in high school, feeling like I didn't belong, the cold weather, not enough to do, too many people who know too much about you.

When you're 18 and itchy, you can come up with a million and a half reasons to escape where you come from, especially if where you come from is a small town.

Grow up in a small town and you pine for a big town. Or at least I did. More things to do. More people to see. More places to go. That's what I wanted, and that's what I got.

I rarely looked back. Over the years, as more and more of my family moved away from Escanaba, my trips back home became more and more infrequent.

And when my dad died last June and I hurried back home, I realized I hadn't been to Escanaba in almost two years.

I missed a lot in his life in those two years. The first time I saw his new apartment was when we went to box up his things after the funeral.

And I never did see the office he had at the courthouse for being a county commissioner. Or the animal shelter where he volunteered so much time that they put up a plaque in his honor after he died.

That's a lot to miss because you're avoiding old pains.

But then we often realize things too late, don't we?

As I continued my walk, the brisk lake breeze brushing my cheek, I wondered: Could I again live here, in Escanaba, in a small town?

The answer surprised me: Probably I could. As I get older, the things that used to bother me about small-town living suddenly seem endearing.

I'd forgotten, for instance, how nice it is not to have to lock your doors. You can do that in small towns. Do that in the big city and you might as well hang a sign on your door: ATTENTION THIEVES. ROB HERE. If you live in the city, you learn to be cautious or else.

I'd also forgotten how slow is the pace in small towns. People drive like they're in no hurry to get somewhere because, usually, they aren't.

They savor time in small towns. Life isn't as much about grabbing, getting and going as it is so often in the big city. It's more often about relationships, getting to know people, enjoying what you have.

In Escanaba, for instance, just about anywhere I go, I know

somebody and they know me. After 15 years.

Amazing.

I've lived places where I didn't know my neighbor's name and he didn't know mine. Why bother when we'd both be moving on again soon?

In small towns they stay put.

In small towns kids grow up in the same house on the same street in the same neighborhood instead of moving around like Army brats and nomads.

In small towns they ask about your mother and your sister and your dog.

In small towns they're quicker to forgive and forget.

At least I hope they are. Because I owe my hometown an apology. It wasn't the problem. I was the problem. I see that now.

Or as the late, great Lewis Grizzard once wrote: "You spend the first half of your life trying to get away from home and the second half trying to get back."

Amen to that, Lewis.

Amen, indeed.

— June 2, 1994

Life
in the
’90s

Updated monikers just confuse

The trouble with this country is we don't call things what they are anymore.

A manhole isn't a manhole anymore. It's a personnel access portal. A used car is pre-owned. A cup holder is a hydration system (this from my stair climber's instruction booklet, which also calls a flat part where you can lay a magazine a "reading center.") A janitor is a sanitation engineer. A waitress is a service provider. A secretary is a personal assistant.

Congressman, policeman, fireman, mailman? Nope. Congressperson, police officer, firefighter, mail deliverer. (Mail? How sexist! Shouldn't that be "deliverable items"?)

We're not even Americans anymore. We've all got labels.

Native American. African-American. Irish American.

Caucasian Yooper American of German and Scottish descent with bad eyes, sore feet and a 15 handicap.

That's me. I'm so proud. My dog, I guess, is a Mutt American. My cat is a Pain-in-the-Butt American.

Stop me, I'm out of control.

Disabled is handicapped. (Or is handicapped disabled?) Fat is horizontally challenged. Short is height impaired. Alcoholics aren't boozers, they're diseased. Drug addicts aren't dopers, they're chemically dependent. Bums aren't bums, they're homeless. Women are womyn. (So why aren't men myn?)

Things aren't broken, they're dysfunctional. We don't

shrink, we downsize. We don't improve, we upgrade. We don't enter, we access. We don't talk, we dialogue.

People aren't jerks, they're insensitive. People aren't crooks, they're victims of a bad upbringing. (Arrest Mom!)

Language evolves, but this is ridiculous. And now it's even getting to our schools.

I have here an article about a local school district that recently built an $11 million high school featuring an "investigation center," an "interaction center," an "expression center," a "competition center" and "exploration centers."

Care to take a guess? When I went to school, we would have called them (in order) libraries, cafeterias, auditoriums, gymnasiums and classrooms. God help us.

"Susie, would you go to the Harvest Moon dance with me in the competition center?"

"Bug off, you sight-impaired, pimple-intensive person of limited social abilities." That means four-eyed, zit-faced creep.

My question is, with all that exploring and investigating going on, when do they get around to "reading" and "writing"? (And for the record, when I was a teen, "exploring" and "investigating" are what we did in the back seat of a Buick with a member of the opposite sex. Now they teach that stuff in class. Go figure.)

This must be some school. What do they call a pencil? A "lead-based communication apparatus"? Is the gym teacher a "competition center enabler"? Is a test a test or is it an "intelligence monitoring system"? And if you flunk it, are you "grade challenged?"

And I wonder: If an adolescent knowledge recipient is caught by an exploration center facilitator throwing a saliva-soaked paper projectile, is he sent to the behavior modification counselor's office for re-education? Or does he merely get his butt paddled in the principal's office?

Some seniors at my high school once gave me a swirlie in a bathroom toilet. What would they call THAT these days?

And, listen, I never wanted to "interact" with the food in my high school cafeteria. I wanted to "not eat it."

Unfortunately, my mother was "bag lunch deficient."

Life was tough then. Today, it's just confusing.

— *November 13, 1994*

Love in '90s governed by policies

Antioch College in Ohio caused a stir the other day with its new sex policy.

The policy, supported by students, says, "Verbal consent should be obtained with each new level of physical and/or sexual contact/conduct in any given interaction regardless of who initiates it."

Makes one wonder, doesn't it, what love will be like in the '90s ...

"Mary."

"Yes, John?"

"Isn't this a wonderful movie?"

"It sure is, John. I love drive-ins."

"Uh, Mary."

"Yes, John?"

"I'd like to ask you something."

"Go ahead, John."

"Well, I, uh, you see, I'd like to put my arm around you."

"Put your arm around me? You mean as in touching me?"

"Yes, I guess so."

"I don't know, John. That would constitute a new level of physical and/or sexual contact/conduct."

"So?"

"So I don't know if I'm prepared to make such an important decision on my own. I feel at this point, it might be wise to consult my psychiatrist."

"Your psychiatrist?"

"The red-haired woman in the back seat. Didn't you wonder who she was?"

"Well, yeah. But I figured she was your sister or something."

"Actually, she's here to make sure I'm emotionally and spiritually ready for such an important step."

"Important step? But it's just an arm. And I used deodorant, honest."

"Look, John, a woman can't be too careful these days. How do I know what you've got in mind?"

"But I don't have anything in mind. I just want to put my arm around you because I think you're pretty."

"Oh, sure. It starts with just an arm around my shoulder. But I know your kind, John."

"My kind?"

"Men, John. You're all alike. First it's an arm around my shoulder, then you'll want to hold my hand, right?"

"Well, maybe."

"And eventually you'd want to kiss me, right?"

"Possibly."

"And we all know where kissing leads to."

"Chapped lips?"

"Sex, John. It leads to sex. And I'm not sure I like you that much."

"Sex? I just want to cuddle with you. If I promise not to do anything more than that, would that be OK?"

"I'm not sure. I'll have to ask my attorney."

"Your attorney?"

"The guy in the suit next to my psychiatrist."

"I wondered who that was."

"He says it's OK if we both sign this consent form."

"Consent form?"

"It's pretty standard, actually. It simply states that we have mutually agreed to the ensuing physical encounter."

"That's not very romantic."

"Romance, schromance. These are the '90s, John. By the way, you'll also have to initial the form at the bottom."

"What for?"

"Your initials indicate that you have read and understand that by agreeing to said physical contact, I have in no way released you from liability in the event that you begin to paw me."

"But, Mary, I'm not going to paw you. I'm a nice guy. Really. I just want to get to know you better."

"And you will. As soon as I see two references."

"References?"

"My lawyer insists, John. He says that you wouldn't hire someone who didn't have references, so why snuggle with them?"

"But I don't have any references with me."

"How about a copy of your latest physical?"

"Huh?"

"My doctor – that's her in the burgundy sweater behind your seat – says I'd be crazy to engage in any kind of physical activity with you if you haven't fully disclosed your medical condition. I mean, how do I know where your arm's been? It could be crawling with diseases."

"Diseases?! I don't have any diseases!"

"Are you yelling at me? Because if you are, I may have to ask my bodyguard to intervene on my behalf."

"Your bodyguard?"

"The big, hairy guy between my lawyer and my psychiatrist."

"This is ridiculous. Look, maybe I should just take you home."

"What, and ruin such a lovely evening?"

— September 26, 1993

Francesca's fantasy falters

"The Bridges of Madison County" one year later:*

"Robert."

"Hmmph?"

"Robert, I'm talking to you."

"What? Can't you see I'm watching a ballgame here?"

"We need to talk, Robert."

"Oh, for cripe's sakes, Francesca. All you ever want to do is talk, talk, talk."

"Oh, Robert, that's exactly what I mean. Conversation used to pour forth from us like wine from twin goblets. Our words twined together like vines on the gates of Bliss. Now the only time we speak is when you leave your toenail clippings on the coffee table."

"If it bothers you so much I'll brush them on the floor, OK. Jeez, what a nag."

"Oh, Robert, what I'm saying is we never talk deeply and passionately about the things that matter anymore."

"You mean like what to watch on TV?"

"No, Robert, I mean like dreams and longings and unfulfilled desires."

"What unfilled desires? You want a new vacuum cleaner or something?"

"You don't see at all, do you? What I miss is the passion."

"What are you talking about? We did it in the La-Z-Boy last night during that commercial, remember?"

"Oh, Robert. That's exactly what I mean. Things have changed between us. Our love used to be like two comets colliding in an ever-blue sky, a cataclysmic communion of rapture and passion."

"It was?"

"Oh, Robert, of course it was. Don't you remember our first four days together? What's happened to you? What's happened to us?"

"Well, you dumped your steady-but-dull farmer husband and married me, and since then we've lived in this here mobile home."

"Oh, Robert, what I'm trying to say is that since our wedding everything is different."

"How so, babe?"

"Well, you quit your job with National Geographic, for one."

"You were always bellyaching about how I was never home. Well, now I'm home. Enjoy."

"But all you do is lie there on the couch watching ballgames on TV and drinking beer. Couldn't you at least go get a job?"

"Listen, hon, there isn't much call for photographers out here in the sticks of Iowa. Besides, we do fine on your paycheck from the Piggly Wiggly. And that reminds me, we're almost out of beer."

"There's another thing."

"What?"

"Your beer consumption. Your belly used to be like a lean, weathered plank from an ocean-going frigate."

"And now?"

"Now it looks like you swallowed a tire."

"Hey!"

"It's true, Robert. You've let yourself go. You've become a different person."

"I have not!"

"Ha! Remember when you used to help with dinner, how I taught you to use a carrot peeler, slowly and sensuously? When's the last time you did that?"

"You kept griping that I didn't do it right!"

"Oh, Robert, and when's the last time we danced?"

"I hate dancing."

"But we danced all the time when first we met!"

"Yeah, but I was courting you then. A guy does all sorts of things he doesn't like to do when he's courting."

"And what happened to letting the day take us wherever it wanted to?"

"Hey, we still do that. Why, just last week I said, 'Honey, how about we let the day take us on down to the fish fry at the Moose Lodge?' "

"Oh, Robert, what I'm trying to say is I long for the days when you would take me in your arms and whisper, 'There are few things in life you know with absolute certainty.' "

"They were just words."

"But beautiful words, Robert. Beautiful, romantic, passionate words."

"You want passionate?"

"Oh, yes, Robert! Yes! More than anything in the world! Pour your passion upon me like milk from a pitcher!"

"OK, how's this: I really, really, REALLY, with all my heart ..."

"Yes, Robert? Yes?"

"... wanna watch this football game. And couldja get me another beer? This one's empty."

"Oh Robert."

—June 19, 1995

Killing us slowly with their news

I have a new theory. Don't worry. It's far better than my last theory, which had the recent tremors in California being caused by bitter, pre-separation wrestling matches between Roseanne and Tom Arnold.

Today's theory is this: Could the Food Nazis be killing us?

Food Nazis are defined as "those who would guilt us out of eating anything that doesn't taste like a stick."

This week, the Center for Science in the Public Interest – sort of the high command of Food Nazism – pronounced Mexican food deadly. Eating it, the organization said, was as suicidal as coughing in front of Dr. Kevorkian.

The list of dangerous foods and ingredients was long and mouthwatering: nachos, enchiladas, tortilla chips, chimichangas, tacos, burritos, guacamole, refried beans, sour cream, cheese.

Which leaves what? Lettuce?

"Hey, Bill, let's go down to Lettuce Bell and get us some endive!"

Somehow it doesn't seem as appealing. But that's the point. Food Nazis love it when we're miserable. They won't be happy until we're all grazing on our lawns.

Oh, sure, in relating this cheery news, Michael Jacobson, the CSPI's executive director in charge of nagging, said, "To those of us who have enjoyed Mexican food, the results are pretty depressing."

But that was play-acting. He's not "depressed" about the news. Food Nazis love it when they can make the rest of us feel rotten. Otherwise why would they do it?

Our best interests? Nah. You'll notice that when Food Nazis proclaim something to be Bad For You, they never say, "But, listen, folks, if you eat this stuff in moderation, it probably won't kill you. Life's a crapshoot, anyway. Might as well enjoy it. Just don't overdo it, OK?"

What they say are things like fettuccine Alfredo is "a heart attack on a plate." Or theater popcorn is "the Godzilla of snacks." Or that chiles rellenos are "the Mexican equivalent of fettuccine Alfredo."

Those are actual quotes from various CSPI spokesnags. Does that sound as if they have our best interest at heart? Or does that sound as if they relish the spotlight and understand exactly how to get it swung their way?

You know what I think. I think Food Nazis, like all fringe types, thrive on attention and a sense of their own power. And in recent years that power has been immense.

When Jacobson's storm troopers did a kamikaze number on Chinese food earlier this year, all but saying that kung pao is Mandarin for "instant death," some Chinese restaurants reported a 50 percent drop in business.

You think Jacobson and his goons didn't enjoy that? They probably whooped "Whee-hee!" and toasted one another with flutes of carrot juice.

And when the same group attacked theater popcorn, millions of moviegoers stopped buying the stuff.

The CSPI's insidious message even got to those of us who kept munching away despite the danger. Each kernel I'd lift to my mouth was accompanied by a nagging, little brain warning: "You're killing yourself, you know. Why not just stick a gun in your mouth and be done with it? Is that a ventricle I hear clogging? Why, I think it is."

And so on. After a while I stopped eating popcorn altogether. Then I decided, "Aw, to heck with it. I only go to the movies once a month anyway, so what's the big deal?"

And I think that attitude is catching on. After each new food scare, I hear more and more people saying, "Who cares? The only thing that's not bad for you is parsley, so what's the difference? I might as well die happy."

In last week's paper, for instance, there was a story about how Americans are fatter than ever. In fact, the study showed a whopping one-third of us are now overweight, up 8 percent since 1980, which is about the time the Food Nazis first started popping up with their studies.

So I got to thinking: Could it be that Americans are increasingly responding to the Food Nazis by eating more and more of the very things that they tell us we shouldn't? Is there an eat-lean backlash going on here?

And if so, does that mean that the Food Nazis, with all their whining and nagging and haranguing, are, in fact, *shortening* our lives rather than extending them?

I don't know about you, but that's my theory, and I'm sticking to it.

— July 24, 1994

Learning too much from trial

I'd heard that if I watched the O.J. Simpson trial I could learn a lot about the American legal system. So I tuned in.

"... Your witness, Mr. Cochran."

"Thank you, Judge Ito. Now Detective Doofus, you told the esteemed prosecuting attorney, Ms. Marcia Frizzy Head over there, that ..."

"Objection, your honor. My hair is not frizzy. If it please the court, my hair has been meticulously sculpted to give me a softer, less intimidating appearance so I don't scare the bejeezus out of the jury."

"Sustained. The jury will ignore the fact that Ms. Clark's hair looks like a fright wig ..."

"Hey!"

"Sorry, Ms. Clark. Please proceed, Mr. Cochran."

"Yes, your honor. You were the first police officer on the crime scene, is that correct, Detective Doofus?"

"Yes, sir."

"So you're saying you got there before anyone else."

"That's correct."

"That would mean, would it not, that no one else got there before you?"

"Yes."

"And that you got there first?"

"Yes! Get on with it already! You're driving me nuts!"

"Your honor, in light of this witness' assertion that he is mentally unstable, I'd like to ask that he be disallowed as a witness in this case."

"Overruled. Proceed."

"All right then, Detective Doofus. When you got to the crime scene, what did you do?"

"I put up yellow police tape to keep people away."

"And this tape, what color is it?"

"Uh, it's yellow."

"And you put it up to keep people 'away,' is that right?"

"Oh, for crying out loud, YES!"

"So what you're saying is this tape was put up by you?"

"Objection, your honor. The defense counsel is being obnoxiously repetitious."

"Objection sustained. The jury is instructed to note that Mr. Cochran is boring the hell out of everyone in this court."

"Sorry, your honor. I was merely trying to be thorough. And may I say that's a very nice tie you're wearing today."

"Objection!"

"What now, Ms. Clark?"

"Defense is sucking up to his honor, your honor. It's not fair, not fair, not fair! WAAA!"

"Overruled. The court can no more tell a lawyer to stop sucking up than it can tell a fish not to swim. Continue, Mr. Cochran."

"Yes, your h— "

RIIIIING

"YEEEE-HAAAAAA!"

"Sorry, your honor. I apologize for my client's outburst. It seems he was just informed that his book hit No. 1 on the best-seller list. If his honor would care to go to sidebar, I'm sure I can persuade my client to provide his honor with an autographed copy."

"Objection! If Mr. Cochran gets to go to sidebar, we do too! And if not, then the entire prosecution team will hold its breath until it turns blue!"

"Relax, Ms. Clark. Call your next witness."

"Thank you, your honor. The prosecution calls The Plaintive Dog."

"Objection! A dog, your honor?"

"What about this, Ms. Clark?"

"The dog is the only true witness to these heinous acts, your honor. Which is why the prosecution has spared no expense bringing in Hugh Airedale, an expert in the field of dog linguistics, to interpret."

"Interpret?"

"Yes, your honor. One woof for no, two for yes."

"Objection! ..."

At this point, I turned off the TV and decided to watch no more. The O.J. trial is indeed a great way to learn about the American legal system.

But I've decided I'd rather not know.

— *February 19, 1995*

Kato is so pathetic we love him

Don't we all have a Kato Kaelin in our lives? By that I mean someone who seems so utterly helpless that he or she is irresistible.

Sure we do. I think that's one reason Kaelin is so popular these days. He's so pathetic you can't help but like him.

Case in point: Last week in court, Robert Shapiro asked Kaelin if Marcia Clark intimidated him? It was a silly question, seeing as how Clark could intimidate a junkyard dog, especially on one of her frequent bad hair days.

But Kaelin seemed almost misty.

"Yes," he snuffled, with that hang-dog look of his. And with that one word, he hooked half the women in America.

My friend Jodie said, "Every woman I know wanted to rush into that courtroom, scoop him up in their arms and protect him. He seemed like such a lost little boy."

Another reason people like him is there's a little Kato in all of us. Who hasn't had a day where the brain fog never lifts and you stumble from task to task, never getting anything right? The difference is, for us it's a temporary condition, whereas with Kato it's apparently permanent. If you heard any of his testimony, you know what I'm talking about.

Clark: "Tell us, Mr. Kaelin, was O.J. furious with Nicole?"

Kato: "Uh, well, sort of. But, um, you know, not really. I guess you'd say ... uh, I don't know if I'd call it, you know, that. It was more, like, I think, some, you know, upsetness."

Upsetness? Oh god, that's so cute and so dumb and so dumbly cute. It's like he's Forrest Gump, only with longer hair and a better tan. How can you not love a guy like that?

You can't. Which is why he's going to be HUGE.

At first, he'll probably make a few guest spots on intellectually challenging TV shows such as "Baywatch."

Kato: "Hey, lifeguard dude, like, which way to the ocean?"

David Hasselhoff: "Uh, it's right there. It's that big blue thing."

Kato: "Cool."

But soon he'll have his own show, probably a one-plot-line type thing where he goes to a grocery store across town in the first episode, becomes hopelessly lost and spends ensuing episodes trying vainly to get home.

Girl: "Look, Mommy, it's a lost man. Can we keep him?"

Mother: "I don't know, dear. He looks like he hasn't had his shots. Plus, how do we know he's really lost?"

Girl: "Are you lost, Mr. Man? Are you sad?"

Kato (his lip quivering): "Upsetness."

And of course there will be endorsements. My mother figures Kato would make a great spokesman for a line of hair care products. "His hair drives me crazy," she says. "It's a wonder a pack of moms hasn't chased him down the block with scissors and shampoo."

There's your commercial right there.

"Get him, Mildred!"

"Quick! Hit him with the cream rinse while he's down!"

"Stay still, Kato dear. This is for your own good."

There will probably even be a Kato action figure. In fact, there will probably be a whole set of O.J. action figures.

It's a natural. You could have an O.J. doll, which would come with a little disguise and a really slow Bronco. The Rosa Lopez doll would have a little plane ticket and a string to pull so she'd say "I don't remember" in Spanish. The Johnnie Cochran doll would, of course, never shut up and have really cool ties. But the Kato doll would be the best.

Wind it up and it would freeload at Ken and Barbie's house.

— April 2, 1995

'King of Road' travels alone these days

I turned the dial.

"... and now, here's 'Erotica' by Madonna ..."

I turned the dial again.

"... I WANNA PUMP, YOOOOOUR BODY! I WANNA JUMP ..."

I turned the dial again.

"... SHAKE YOUR BAH-DAY, UHH! SHAKE YOUR BAH-DAY ..."

I dialed clear around the FM dial. Everywhere the sound was enough to make my ears gnash their teeth. Prince screaming about sex. Rappers screaming about sex. Heavy metal groups just screaming. (Probably about sex, but who can tell?)

Annoyed, I switched to AM. AM radio still has a shred of sanity left to it these days. I tuned in a news program. "... singer/songwriter Roger Miller, dead at the age of ..."

Perfect.

Popular music's gone to hell, and now one of my heroes from a time when music was something special, not just something to mate to, is gone.

If you are under 30, maybe you don't remember Roger Miller. I do. He came up with one of my all-time favorite songs, "King of the Road," plus some other pretty cool stuff.

He was from what I guess you'd call the old school. He didn't shake his groove thang. In fact, I don't think he even had one. He didn't scream. He never made a video, to my knowledge. And I'm quite certain he never wore nothing but his underwear on stage. Also, the closest he ever got to writing a profane lyric was "Dang me."

He sang songs. That's it. He just sang songs. It seems like hardly anybody does that anymore, and I miss it.

I know I sound like my parents when I say this, but I happen to think I'm not alone in believing that popular music today stinks.

I don't know what happened to it. It was great in the '60s. It was great in the '70s. Then in the '80s it began to slide.

Now it's 1992, and, at the ripe old age of 31, I look at a list of the Top 10 and realize I don't know any of the songs. And I don't want to.

Call me a young fogey, but most of the songs on the radio today sound the same to me. There's a booming bass. There's a screaming guitar. There's a screeching singer. And that's it. No lyrics of much interest or consequence. No melody. Nothing clever whatsoever. It's no wonder there are so many remakes of old hits these days.

And now Roger Miller's gone, God and Elvis rest his soul. The newspapers said he died of cancer. He was only 56.

Somehow I thought he was older, maybe because he was one of my dad's favorites. Dad put all his favorites in the jukebox.

Where he got the jukebox, I don't know, but it looked exactly like the one on the opening of "Happy Days," and it was filled with great old songs of the '50s and '60s, like "Chattanooga Choo-Choo," "The Good, the Bad and the Ugly" and "Down in the Boondocks."

My favorite, though, was D-18 – "King of the Road."

There was something about the song. The jazzy bass solo it began with. The cool-cat finger-snaps. The melody. Miller's laid-back voice.

And then there were those lyrics:

> *Trailer for sale or rent; rooms to let, 50 cents;*
> *No phone, no pool, no pets. Ain't got no cigarettes;*
> *Ah, but two hours of pushing broom,*
> *buys an 8-by-12 four-bit room;*
> *I'm a man of means by no means, King of the Road.*

Let's see Prince write stuff like that. Even if he could, he'd probably squeal the words so badly you couldn't recognize them. Plus, he'd grab his crotch while doing so, which, come to think of it, may be why he squeals so much in the first place.

But back to Roger. When I heard he'd died, I realized I didn't own any of his music, so I went to the store.

I came back with "Roger Miller's Golden Hits." It's got all the good stuff: "Dang Me," "You Can't Roller Skate in a Buffalo Herd," "Do-Wacka-Do" and, of course, "King of the Road."

I've played that song so much the grooves may collapse. My favorite part is when ol' Roger gets to the line about smoking "old stogeys I have found, short but not too big around."

That's what's so great about this song: You hear it, and a part of you wants to live it. You want to ride rails and head for Bangor, Maine, wild and free. And you want to do it just the way Roger sings it.

You want the third boxcar on a midnight train, and to hell with paying union dues.

— November 8, 1992

Halloween '93 is truly scary and sensitive

*alloween in the '90s ...*

"Mommy."

"Yes, Junior?"

"I've decided what I want to be for Halloween."

"That's nice, Junior."

"I'm going to be a hobo."

"I see."

"What's wrong, Mommy?"

"Well, dear, Mommy is just a little concerned."

"Why, Mommy?"

"Because hobos are homeless people, dear."

"So."

"So you wouldn't want everyone to think you are insensitive to the plight of the homeless, would you?"

"I guess not. But Daddy was a hobo when he was my age."

"That was a long time ago, dear. We're much more enlightened these days. Maybe you should pick something else."

"OK, maybe I'll be one of the Seven Dwarfs."

"A dwarf?"

"Yeah, like in 'Snow White.' I wanna be Dopey."

"Well, dear, Mommy is sorry to tell you this, but she has two teensy little problems with you being a dwarf."

"What problems?"

"One, she's not comfortable with a costume that makes fun

of the vertically challenged."

"The what?"

"Short people, dear. And two, Mommy thinks Dopey might have had a substance abuse problem."

"A what?"

"Never mind, dear. Pick something else."

"OK, how about an Indian?"

"You mean a Native American."

"A what?"

"Indians are called Native Americans these days, dear. And, yes, you can dress up like one, as long as your costume reflects a multicultural, nonstereotypical view of Native Americans."

"A what?"

"No war paint, dear."

"But that's no fun. How about if I go as a gangster?"

"That's fine."

"Great!"

"As long as you don't carry a toy gun."

"But how am I going to be a gangster without a gun?"

"I don't know, dear, but Mommy and Daddy are strongly against violence of any kind."

"OK. Maybe I'll just be a pumpkin then."

"That's a wonderful idea, Junior. But remember, be home by 6 o'clock."

"Why do I have to be home by 6?"

"Because it gets dark at 6, and I don't want you out after dark."

"But that's the whole point of Halloween. You go out in the dark and do stuff. How am I going to soap old man Miller's windows when it's light out?"

"You're not, dear. Soaping someone's windows isn't nice. Besides, he might mistake you for a robber and shoot you."

"Shoot me?!"

"Homeowners can't be too careful these days, son. There's an awful lot of crime out there."

"Well, can I at least toilet paper the Johnson's tree?"

"I'm afraid not, Junior. Doing so would be ecologically unsound, not to mention the fact that if Mr. Johnson sees you he might ..."

"Shoot me?"

"Exactly."

"Well, how about if I let the air out of Mrs. Smith's tires?"

"Not unless you want a good spanking, young man. Plus, you might set off her car alarm."

"But if I can't play tricks on anybody, what can I do?"

"Why, you can do anything you like, dear, as long as you stay on our block and promise not to go up to that blue house on the corner."

"Why can't I trick-or-treat at the blue house on the corner?"

"Because it's a crack house, dear."

"A what?"

"A crack house is a place where they ... look, just don't go there, OK? And remember to bring your bag of candy home before you eat any."

"What for?"

"So we can take it down to the police station to have it X-rayed."

"X-rayed?"

"So we can see if any of our neighbors put any pins or bits of glass into your candy."

"But why would they do that?"

"I wish I knew, dear."

"OK, OK, I'll bring home the candy. Is there anything else I should do or remember?"

"Only one more thing."

"What's that, Mommy?"

"Have fun out there, dear."

— October 28, 1993

'Make my day' should end with please

If you want to know how truly nutty this country has become, all you have to do is look at a recent column by Judith Martin, the nationally syndicated columnist who goes by the name Miss Manners.

It began this way:

"DEAR MISS MANNERS: When my little Johnny wishes to play at Jimmy's house, how do I ask Jimmy's parents if they keep firearms, and if so, whether they store them in a locked cabinet?

"If I am giving a large party with many guests who are casual acquaintances, is there a polite way to remind everyone of the concealed-weapons law in my jurisdiction? Or do I just have to hope?

"I have no wish to use etiquette as a basis for proselytizing and am most anxious to avoid acrimonious debate with those who may be heavily armed."

In case you're wondering, the letter is real. I know because I called United Features Syndicate in New York and spoke to Linda Bossen, who edits the Miss Manners column.

Said Bossen: "She does get letters from time to time ... that sound as if the writer of the letter was not entirely serious. But I have a feeling that this letter is genuine."

It probably came, she said, from a reader who lives in an area where the crime rate is high and people are arming themselves for protection.

Which, these days, could be anywhere, I mentioned.

"It is sort of depressing, isn't it?" said Bossen.

Yes, it is. It's also depressing that guns have become such an accepted part of normal everyday life that they have become fodder for an etiquette column. The suggestion seems to be: We apparently have to live with them, so we may as well live with them in a civilized manner.

One can only imagine the letters that await etiquette columnists in the future. With deepest apologies to the inimitable Miss M., we present:

DEAR MANNERS GUY: I am hosting a formal dinner party, but I am terribly confused about something. Is it customary to leave a spot in the place settings for the handguns of dinner guests?

GENTLE READER: Indeed, it is. Manners Guy suggests leaving space at the far end of the utensils on the right side of the plate, as most people are right-handed. Such placement allows easier access to the weapon in the event that the soup is cold or the host overfills the water glass.

DEAR MANNERS GUY: I was in the express checkout lane at the supermarket the other day when I noticed the woman in front of me had what looked to be too many items. I told her to move to an appropriate checkout, but she refused, so I flashed her my .357 Magnum, which caused her to rethink her position. Now I'm worried: Was my behavior gauche?

GENTLE READER: No, it would have been gauche had you fired. The noise may have greatly disturbed the other shoppers.

DEAR MANNERS GUY: Help! I'm in love with a woman in my place of business, but am too shy to approach her. I'm into guns and from what I can tell so is she. So I'm thinking about buying her a Saturday Night Special as a way of saying, "Would you be mine?" Is this too forward of me?

GENTLE READER: Gifts of introduction, while dated, are a noble custom and Manners Guy heartily endorses them. However, he is concerned at your choice of firearms. As any gangbanger can tell you, a Saturday Night Special is short on both caliber and accuracy and is therefore more likely to convey the message, "Would you be mine for the evening?" Manners Guy suggests a firearm of substantially higher quality and firepower.

DEAR MANNERS GUY: Is it OK to wear white holsters after Labor Day?

GENTLE READER: What does Manners Guy look like, a fashion columnist? He suggests you ask someone who cares.

DEAR MANNERS GUY: Could you settle an argument for me? My husband and I were in a fast-food establishment when a gunman entered and demanded money from the cashier. I say the man was very rude in that he didn't preface his demand by saying "please." Nor did he say "thank you" when the transaction was completed. My husband claims normal rules of courtesy are null and void in a stick-up situation. I say he's crazy. Who's right?

GENTLE READER: You are. The gunman, although rushed, should have followed the established rules of courtesy. Remember: Manners are the hallmark of a civilized society.

—September 19, 1993

Skinny shot may not be good news

Everyone seems convinced that the latest study, in which scientists found a hormone that caused mice to lose weight rapidly, is a good thing.

One scientist said, "This is perhaps the major finding in the field of obesity in the last two decades."

And my friend Flounder, the human pizza, said: "There is a God."

What they did is inject genetically obese mice with the hormone, which increased their metabolisms and dampened their appetites, causing the pounds to melt away, the result being mice that looked like Kate Moss, only with bigger ears.

A similar hormone is said to exist in humans as well, so the thinking is that someday you and I will be able to suck down all the Big Macs and Ben & Jerry's we want, then shuffle off to the doctor for a skinny shot.

Great news, right? Not so fast, Twinkie lips. There are a few things we haven't considered here.

First of all, these experiments were conducted on mice, not people. If we believed mice studies, we'd be reduced to consuming nothing but oat bran and yak milk because everything else, especially anything that tastes good, seems to give those stupid rodents cancer.

Second, how do they know it was the hormone that caused Mickey and Minnie to lose weight? Maybe they simply did a few hundred extra turns on their exercise wheel when the scientists weren't looking. Or maybe mice are as vain as people and they reset the scales before they were weighed. Mice are crafty that way.

And then there's this: According to what I read, the study was conducted at something called the Howard Hughes Medical Institute in California. What, you're going to believe scientific findings from a place named after a guy with 8-inch toenails? Not me, cottage-cheese thighs.

But, OK, let's say the study holds up. Is that good news?

Maybe not. For one thing, a fat-shedding shot would ruin the billion-dollar diet industry in this country. Who would want to choke down all that low-fat, low-taste gunk they make you eat when they could get a shot and live on Oreos?

Think of the ramifications. Jenny Craig would be forced to find some other body flaw on which to make money – say, big ears: "Do people call you Dumbo? Join Jenny Craig!"

Weight Watchers would probably become Height Watchers, for people who consider themselves too tall.

Then there are all the aerobics instructors. What'll happen to them? Who's going to work out if medical science can save them the trouble? Thousands of aerobics instructors will be out of work. I can see it now: Cities great and small will be beset by extremely chipper beggars in leotards and Spandex.

Brrr.

And then there's this – with no chubby guts to shrink, Richard Simmons and Susan Powter would be out there looking for work. Meaning: THEY MIGHT END UP WORKING IN YOUR OFFICE!!! Now that's scary.

Farmers, too, would be hurt by a fat-busting drug. Would anyone ever eat broccoli, watercress or spinach again? And who would drink diet pop? The NutraSweet and Sweet 'N Low people would go out of business overnight. We'd also be up to our ears in uneaten rice cakes, fat-free chips and tofu.

People would spend their days running from one fast-food joint to another. Gluttony would become the national hobby. Why, even Jane Fonda would be tempted to say, "Aw, what the hell, pass the doughnuts."

A scientific breakthrough?

I think not, Cheetos breath.

— August 6, 1995

Remove 'V' from TV and what's left?

I plan to be first in line to get a V-chip television, if and when they come about.

A V-chip, in case you aren't aware, is not something that goes great with V-dip. It's a device that someday soon will be built into TV sets across the land to block out objectionable programming.

The government says we desperately need these chips so kids don't see all the sex and violence out there.

Fine. Great. Protect the kids. But what about us adults? I can think of *lots* of things I wish wouldn't get into my TV set.

For starters, how about TV news? There's nothing more violent, lurid or depressing on TV than the news. Plus, do we really need 10 minutes of weather or that inane happy talk the anchors make before going to commercial?

I don't think so. I'd definitely V-chip the news.

I'd also V-chip all soap operas. My wife loves them, but I'm sorry, I think they're dumb. Someone named Steele is always messing around with someone named Brooke, who has just broken up with Antonio because he stabbed Alec after catching him in bed with Nikki, who was Sergio's girlfriend before that snake Stone wooed her away after she regained her memory following a bout of amnesia brought on by the shock of finding her lover Vlad in bed with her pool man, Chad, and his Doberman, Killer.

You want to know the reason none of the characters on a

soap opera appears to have a job? It's because they're all too busy sleeping with one another. Pandas should mate so often.

I'd also block MTV. I used to like it when they showed actual music videos, but near as I can tell they rarely do that anymore. And the ones they *do* air are by bands with names like The Horny Tree Frogs or Belch and the Body Odors.

I could live without VH-1, too, since all it plays anymore are videos by my sworn enemy Michael Bolton, who sings like his rubber underwear is too tight. Plus that mane of his makes him look like the Cowardly Lion. You ever notice that?

I'd block C-Span. I don't want to see my government make laws any more than I want to see how they turn a cow into steak. Plus there's too much sex and violence in politics these days.

What else? Ah, yes, I'd definitely like to see a Sam Donaldson chip, just because his hair is so bizarre I can't pay attention to anything he's saying.

There should be a Sally Struthers chip, too. Sure, I want to help starving children, but she's whinier now than she was back on "All in the Family," and I hate whining.

And if there is a chip devoted to blocking Sally Struthers, there certainly ought to be one blocking Richard Simmons, who is high on my list of The Most Annoying People on the Planet. (I think his problem is he drinks too much coffee.)

Infomercials. Chip them, too. Let Cher find honest work.

Ditto for those home shopping channels. I don't need a commemorative Elvis plate or a cubic zirconia ring. Nobody does.

I'd block all nature programs, too. How many times can you watch a lion kill an antelope?

In fact, I would V-chip all commercials, all stand-up comedians, all sitcoms, all reruns and all old movies starring anyone other than John Wayne or Clint Eastwood.

Which leaves what?

Well, there's still ESPN, which is my favorite station because I love sports. Problem is my wife would almost certainly want that one blocked.

So maybe I'll forget about buying a V-chip TV and buy a radio instead.

— September 11, 1995

Tawdry is in talk show beholders' eyes

Posing as a Former Male Stripper Whose Gender-Confused Border Collie Is Having an Affair With His Gay Neighbor's Sexually Repressed Iguana, I snuck into the Talk Show Summit last weekend in New York.

Here's an exclusive look at what transpired:

SALLY: "Ladies, gentlemen and Geraldo ..."

GERALDO: "Hey!"

SALLY: " ... as you know, our industry is at a major crossroads."

MAURY: "Did she say cross-dressers?"

PHIL: "I love cross-dressers! Instant ratings!"

MONTEL: "You're telling me. I had these cross-dressers on once who ..."

SALLY: "Crossroads, you morons, not cross-dressers! What's the matter with you? Haven't you been hearing all the criticism lately?"

CHARLES: "Criticism? Darn it, I knew that show on 'Nursing Home Hookers' was too mild. Don't worry, Sally, I'll do better!"

MONTEL: "And I'll punch up my show on 'Sluts in Cyberspace!' "

CARNIE: "And I can, like, have my 'Skinhead Grade School Teachers' throw chairs at each other and stuff!"

SALLY: "People! I'm talking about the criticism that our shows are too lurid, too sensational, too irresponsible! Any thoughts on that?"

RICKI: "Uh, yeah, does anyone know how I can get hold of the 'Siamese Twins Who Are Dating Themselves'?"

CHARLES: "I do! I'll swap you their number for those modern-day vegetarian vampires you had on last week."

RICKI: "Deal! But you have to throw in that guy who's divorcing his wife but wants to keep dating her breast implants."

PHIL: "Hey, I was gonna do him next! Right after my show on the woman who's marrying her Shih Tzu."

CARNIE: "Can you say Shih Tzu on TV?"

SALLY (whistling): "PWEEET! People, please, you're not listening! We've got a problem! No less than Donna Shalala is upset with us."

JENNY: "Donna Shalala. Say, isn't she the 'Woman Who Weighs More Than a Mack Truck'? "

JERRY: "No, I think she was 'I Was My Boss' Sex Slave ... and I Liked It' "

SALLY: "You ninnies, Donna Shalala is none other than the Secretary of Health and Human Services!"

GERALDO: "A secretary? What's she gonna do, make us coffee?"

MAURY: "Haw! Good one, Geraldo!"

CARNIE: "Knock it off, you guys. Sally's, like, trying to tell us about her, like, secretary. Go ahead, Sally."

SALLY: "Donna Shalala happens to be part of the Clinton administration."

RICKI: "Oh. My. Gawd. You mean she wants to admit to an illicit affair with the big man himself? Is that it?!"

JENNY: "Dibs!"

SALLY (sighing): "No. She said that we should 'ethically as professionals and morally as citizens stop showcasing the raunchy and ridiculous.' "

GERALDO: "Ethically and morally? I'm sorry, Sal-gal, but you've lost me there. Darn it, woman, speak English."

SALLY: "She further said, and I quote, 'We lose when we spotlight absurd, antisocial or even violent behavior and portray it as a norm.' "

JENNY: "You mean like 'Cooks Who Hock Loogies in the Deep-Fry'?"

MAURY: "Or 'He Talks to My Cleavage, Should My Cleavage

Talk Back?' "

SALLY: "Exactly. We must rise above this sort of programming. We must uplift the people!"

MONTEL: "I get it! You mean like a show on the Wonderbra!"

SALLY: "No, what I mean is we must give viewers what they need and not what they want."

RICKI: "You mean I shouldn't do 'I Inseminated Myself With a Baster and Now I Feel Like a Turkey'?"

SALLY: "Precisely!"

RICKI: "Or 'I Fell in Love With My Blow-Up Doll but She Thinks I'm an Airhead'?"

SALLY: "Yes! You've got it!"

RICKI: "But that show drew a 30 share."

EVERYONE (in unison): "A 30 SHARE?"

RICKI: "Right."

SALLY (whispering): "Uh, say, you wouldn't still have that guy's number, would you?"

RICKI: "Sure!"

PHIL: "Hey, wait a minute. What about all that stuff about responsibility and dignity?"

SALLY: "Eat dirt, grandpa. For a 30 share, I'd do a show on 'Talk Show Hosts Who Eat Their Young.' "

—November 2, 1995

No home computer for this guy

Twenty-two reasons why I don't own a home computer and probably never will unless I have a daughter who grows up to marry Bill Gates' grandson:

1. If I got one, all I would do is play tank games, and I waste too much time doing stupid stuff already.

2. I don't need a $3,000 machine to balance my checkbook. That's what my wife is for, and all I have to do is keep her fed.

3. Last month, world chess champ Garry Kasparov almost lost to Deep Blue, a super computer. That's too scary for words. (Note to Kasparov: Next time, if the match gets close, spill a glass of water on its keyboard. *Viva la humans!*)

4. I stare at a computer screen all day at work. Why would I want to stare at one all night too?

5. It bugs me that E-mail addresses consist of long strings of gobbledygook like ash.//$@geekboy./***http. Why can't they use street addresses and zip codes like the rest of us? (The answer: Computer people can't resist making easy things difficult.)

6. It's because of computers that we have telephone voice mail systems, which are in the Top 10 as far as most annoying inventions ever (also in the Top 10: fruit-on-the-bottom yogurt, car telephones and Newt Gingrich).

7. If I bought a computer my 2-year-old son would probably learn to operate the thing before I do, and I'd at least like him to be in grade school before he realizes he's

smarter than me.

8. I can't operate my VCR. How am I going to run a computer?

9. I dated a computer science major in college who wouldn't let me interface with her databases, and I still haven't gotten over it.

10. If I want to play solitaire, I'll use a deck of cards, thank you very much.

11. To me a megabyte is something you get from a byg dog.

12. Computer users call a period a "dot." That's dumb.

13. I asked the computer person here at work to teach me how to send E-mail from the office Mac since I get a lot of E-mail messages from readers and it would be nice to reply. She said, "Sure, it's simple," then proceeded to give me a list of instructions longer than my arm. All this to send a message saying "Thanks." I could hand-deliver a letter faster.

14. I can't get over the feeling that if I buy a computer it will be obsolete within six months, and I'll have to buy another one and so on, and I went through that whole rigamarole already with 8-tracks, cassettes and CDs.

15. If I buy a computer I might start talking like a geek, as in: "When I tried to download the database off my CD-ROM the system crashed and I blew a gigabyte on my hard drive."

16. They call that thing you move with your hand a mouse. My wife hates mice.

17. It's because of computers that the word "access" became a verb.

18. A woman I know says she keeps her to-do lists on her computer, which cost $2,000. I told her I keep my lists on a pad of paper, which cost 49 cents. And paper never crashes.

19. Another woman I know said her computer allows her to communicate with people all over the country. I said, "So does my telephone."

20. I'm afraid to merge onto the information superhighway with Yugo skills.

21. Computers are trendy, and I've always prided myself on being a maverick. This way I get to act all snooty and superior.

22. My wife won't let me.

— March 17, 1996

The day downsizing was done

Ebenezer Scrooge IV, corporate CEO ...

"Cratchit, get in here."

"Yes, sir, Mr. Scrooge."

"Mrs. Scrooge maxed out my credit cards again. Do you know what this means, Cratchit?"

"Yes, sir. It means you're going to give yourself another obscenely large raise."

"That's right! And how am I going to free up money to do that?"

"Layoffs, sir. Massive, sweeping, family-crippling layoffs."

"Hee! Hee! Right again, dear boy. I do so love being a CEO. But if I've told you once, Cratchit, I've told you a thousand times – the preferred term these days is downsize."

"I'll remember that, sir."

"Good. Now I think 100 workers ought to do it. Send out pink slips immediately."

"We can't, sir."

"Can't isn't in my vocabulary, Cratchit. How do you think I got to be CEO of Scrooge Amalgamated Worldwide Inc.?"

"I believe your father gave you the job. And his father gave him the job before that. And he got it from your great-grandfather, the original Scrooge."

"Blast you, Cratchit. I meant besides that!"

"By having a heart four sizes too small?"

"That's the Grinch, Cratchit! Now stop with the wisecracks

and issue those pink slips immediately!"

"As I said, sir, we can't. There's a problem."

"A problem?"

"Yes, sir. We don't have a hundred employees left, sir."

"We don't?"

"No, sir. Don't you remember? You laid off 5,000 people back in 1990 so you could build mansions in Tuscany, Tokyo and Timbuktu."

"Ah, yes."

"And then in '95, the board said they would triple your stock options if you trimmed the fat, so you fired all the middle managers."

"And right at Christmas, too! What memories!"

"And then last month you laid off the entire marketing, planning and development departments to drive up our stock price on Wall Street."

"By gum, that was a stroke of genius, wasn't it? Increasing profits by shrinking the company! Who'd have thought we'd see the day! I tell you, Cratchit, I love the '90s!"

"And finally, on Monday, you downsized another 500 people."

"Ah, yes. I was in a foul mood after losing that polo match Sunday. So tell me, Cratchit, exactly how many employees do we have left?"

"Two, sir."

"Is that all?"

"Yes, sir. Just you and me."

"Hmm. That would explain why the parking lot has been so empty lately."

"And why the production lines have stopped."

"The production lines have stopped? Good grief, that's terrible! Get down there and start them up immediately, Cratchit!"

"I could, sir, but I doubt it will do any good."

"What are you blathering about, Cratchit?"

"With all due respect, sir, there's so much downsizing going on in America these days there's hardly anybody left who can afford to buy our products."

"I see. Well, there's only one thing to do, then."

"What's that, sir?"

"You're fired, Cratchit."

"But, sir, Tiny Tim needs braces!"

"And I need a new yacht. So you know what that means, don't you, Cratchit?"

"Bah humbug, sir?"

"Bah humbug, Cratchit."

— March 25, 1996

How to flush out wacky researchers

A recent news story has led me to the belief that we need extremely stiff penalties for scientists and researchers who scare the public without knowing what they're talking about.

The story concerned toilets. A few years ago, a University of Arizona scientist named Charles Gerba published a study that said when you flush the toilet, little bits of fecal material fly into the air and get all over everything. Including nearby toothbrushes.

I remember reading about this study. It scared me to death, as I am highly and regrettably susceptible to believing things I read in print, no matter how bizarre.

So I ended up worrying, "Toilet water? Fecal material? Good grief, I might as well brush my teeth with the toilet scrubber!"

Sure, toilet water never seems to do dogs any harm, but then I had a dog once whose favorite restaurant was Chez Litter Box.

I worried so much about this study that I kept my toothbrush in a drawer thereafter. And even then a small part of me was unnerved. I would look at my toothbrush in the morning and wonder what other microscopic creepy crawlies were on there. Brushing was never the same after that.

Now, of course, I learn that I had nothing to fear. Another study now says the earlier study is full of fecal material. It said toilet germs don't go airborne, as previously thought.

They go down the drain. End of story.

So once again we've been duped. This happens too often these days. Some scientist who wants to see his name in print studies something that no one ever thought to worry about before, discovers something horrifying and writes a paper on it for some medical journal, which is then picked up by the media. And before you know it, we're all fretting about Chinese food. Or Mexican food. Or wine (now considered beneficial; I'll drink to that!) Or air bags (said to have injured a few small children; forget how many they've saved). Or global warming (It was hard to concentrate on this frightening prospect this past winter and spring, what with all the snow.)

Or, worse, we're gulping down dreadful junk like oat bran because some near-sighted test-tube sniffer says it will suck cholesterol out of our systems faster than Dom DeLuise sucks the filling out of cannoli.

Then, a year later, you can count on another study contradicting the first, which is the scientific equivalent of saying, "Whoops."

And what happens to the moron who was proven wrong?

Nothing. He already got his publicity and the resulting research grant. He's happier than a pig in the aforementioned toilet material. He couldn't care less that he caused millions of people needless worry.

That, my friends, is not right. There oughta be a law. You can't yell "fire!" in a public building if there isn't a fire. Nor should you be able to say, "Watch out, toilet cooties!"

I propose the following. I say any researcher who ballyhoos a scary study that later turns out to be false be tried and found guilty of first degree worry inducement.

A fitting punishment might be having a hypnotist implant frightening but erroneous beliefs into the the accused's brain for the same length of time that he or she made the public worry. These beliefs could be something such as tap water causes cancer or blinking causes blindness.

Or in Mr. Gerba's case, we could implant the thought that toilet seats have teeth and a huge appetite for bare backsides.

He'd never go in peace again.

How fitting indeed.

— June 2, 1996

Critters

Sappy or not, pets bring out a special love

A colleague asked me what I was going to write about today, and I said old dogs.

He wrinkled his nose. "Too sappy," is what he was thinking.

He's probably right. Old dogs is a sappy topic. But I don't care.

Murphy is dying.

He's my father's dog, a stub-tailed springer spaniel with a foghorn for a bark, a rolled-up fire hose for a tongue and the purest heart you'd ever want to see.

The two are best buddies, especially since the divorce. They hunt together, watch TV together, go for walks together. I don't know if he still does it, but Dad even used to fix Murphy his own toast in the morning.

With butter.

And if Dad ever forgot, Murphy would remind him by sitting next to his chair and whining, as if to say, "Hey, Dad, how about some toast? And don't skimp on the butter this time."

Dad called me with the news the other day. His voice was ragged at the edges, so I knew something was wrong.

Murphy had been the same as always – meaning a slobbering, oafish, utterly lovable galoot – then, boom, all of a sudden he wouldn't eat or drink.

And this is a dog that lives for eating. He'll eat anything, anytime, in whatever amount he can get.

I bought him one of those huge rawhide bones once, the ones dogs gnaw on endlessly. He ate it. It didn't seem to do him any harm though. I'm sure he simply washed it down with a gigantic swig from the toilet, had himself a good burp, then went looking for something else to eat.

Springer spaniels are like that. I used to kid Dad about whether he was raising a horse or a dog.

"A pig," he'd say. And we'd laugh. And now ol' Murph is dying. A veterinarian friend diagnosed him as having a large, cancerous tumor wrapped around his spleen.

Operating, she told my dad, would probably kill Murphy. But without surgery, he probably wouldn't last a month. It was up to my dad.

He chose to get some painkillers for Murphy and let him live out whatever days he has left in relative peace.

That was last week. The medicine helped. Murphy is "banging around," as my dad says. He's even got his appetite back. So for now, he's fine.

I'm not so sure about my dad.

You can tell he's deeply hurt. No wonder. Losing a dog is tough. I remember every single dog my family owned and how awful I felt when they died.

Lassie was the first one. Great dog. Looked just like the original Lassie.

Some people think collies are high-strung and aloof, but they probably never owned one. Lassie was gentle and patient and had the richest, thickest fur in the world. I still remember the feel of it against my cheek.

She somehow got out one night. From the living room we heard the thud and her cry of pain. We were watching "My Three Sons."

That was 25 years ago. I still think of her when I see that show.

Samantha was another great dog. She was a cockapoo, and although she was small and had to scramble to keep up, she loved walking with me on my morning paper route, even in the deepest snows and on the coldest mornings.

It killed her eventually. One winter morning she got hold of some poisoned meat a man along my route put out because he didn't like dogs in his yard.

The police couldn't do anything. No proof. So the next summer, Stan Venne and I smoke-bombed his house. We didn't need proof. We knew.

I know it was a rotten thing to do, but we were kids and I loved that dog. I'd had her a long time, and dogs you have a long time are the hardest to lose.

Old dogs are like that. Even if they just lie there like a piece of furniture, slobber on everything and smell bad, you love them just the same.

You may not be able to teach old dogs new tricks, but neither can you teach young dogs how to be old dogs.

Old dogs are irreplaceable. When they die, part of you dies.

That's why I feel so bad for my dad.

Murphy isn't exactly old. He is 8, which is really just middle-aged in dog years. But he's close enough. He has that comfortable old-shoe quality.

He's got another couple of weeks.

I'm sure Dad will be making a lot of toast.

— May 11, 1992

Dogged into going to dentist

Today we are going to discuss a subject that's no doubt constantly on your mind: dog breath, specifically that of my dog, Garfunkel.

To put it bluntly, it stinks.

I knew you'd care.

My dog's veterinarian says the best way to give him fresh, minty breath is to bring him into the office to have his teeth professionally cleaned.

I don't know. First of all, I'd have to get him into the car, which usually isn't a problem. Garfunkel feels as strongly about riding in the car as he does about conducting impromptu late-night barking jams with the dog across the street.

Normally, all we have to do is open the car door and say, "Get ..." whereupon Garfunkel zooms into the car and busies himself with the crucial dog job of running hysterically from front to back and wiping his drippy nose on the windows.

But, and you pet owners know what I'm talking about here, pets can somehow sense, through air vibrations or something, when a car trip to the vet is imminent.

Garfunkel's response is to hide under our bed until we flush him out with (in his 4-watt mind) the Vacuum Cleaner Attachment From Hell.

Once he's out, I attempt to pick him up, which, naturally, is his cue to make himself suddenly weigh 300 pounds.

How dogs do this is one of life's great mysteries, right up there with what Phyllis Diller ever did to become famous.

Anyway, when we finally get him in the car, he decides it's time to go into Hyperactive Trembling, Shedding, Whining, Panting, Acting Like Jack Nicholson in "One Flew Over the Cuckoo's Nest" Mode. So, you can see, this is no fun.

Secondly, aside from wondering how the vets get the animals to rinse and spit, I'm a little suspicious of this whole doggie dentistry thing.

My vet tells me it's the coming wave in veterinary medicine. He says there is a veritable plethora of dental services and products for dogs and cats these days. He says (and I am not making this up) you can get everything from meat-flavored toothpastes and mouthwashes to braces, gold teeth and overbite cures. Here's what I say: "What? No designer toothpicks? No WaterPiks? No doggy dentures or kitty caps?"

Because, to be honest with you, I don't want my dog to go to the dentist and come home with a better smile than me. And I certainly don't want him hogging the bathroom every morning while he brushes and flosses. (God knows the hair HE'D leave in the sink.)

Besides, it's not like he needs to do these things to improve his social life or anything. This is a creature, after all, whose entire social life consists of rushing up to other dogs and sniffing their privates.

All I really want is to be able to eat dinner without Garfunkel's breath curling my nostril hairs. Is that too much to ask? I don't think so.

But when I suggested to my vet that I simply buy the dog a pack of Certs or something, he launched into one of those long, boring speeches about dental hygiene and its link to overall health and how would I like it if I never had my teeth cleaned (fine, actually) and blah, blah, blah.

So, OK, maybe I'll have the dumb dog's dumb teeth cleaned. And maybe I'll even let the doc check him out for any other dental problems. But there are going to be some rules.

If that dog needs a retainer to correct an overbite and I buy him one and he loses it, I'm sorry, that's it, it's coming out of his allowance.

— May 31, 1990

Only a dog? Mutt was much more

We had Garfunkel put down the other day. It was one of the hardest things we've ever done.

Marcia lifted him onto the shiny metal table, held him tight one last time, the veterinarian moved in, and a few seconds later Garf was gone.

Marcia cried. I patted her shoulders.

The house has felt empty since. He was not just a dog. He was part of the family, a part of our lives. But it had to be done. That's what we keep telling ourselves.

Marcia had him for 17 years. I knew him for 14 of those years, the first two of which he growled at me, as he did at all her suitors. Eventually, though, he accepted me, and Marcia considered that enough of an endorsement to marry me.

"He's a good judge of character," she explained.

And he was. He barked daily at the postman, probably because he knew those were bills that were being delivered. And he howled with rage whenever he saw squirrels, which he was forever chasing and forever not catching.

I hate bill deliverers and squirrels, too. So I would punish him for these outbursts by saying, "Good boy."

He was a good dog. Always full of vigor and light.

Then about 18 months ago, he had a stroke. He couldn't stand, much less walk. His eyes raced back and forth as if he were watching a high-speed pingpong match. His hearing and sight suffered.

But with medicine and love, he was soon back to being the same hairy, smelly, cat food stealer he'd always been.

We were thrilled. We felt like he'd cheated death. After all, he was 16 at the time. How many dogs live to be 16, much less survive a major stroke?

Then, a month ago, his luck – and our luck – ran out. Marcia heard a thud in the night – Garfunkel had collapsed and couldn't get up – and we knew it had happened again.

We took him to the vet, who gave us more medicine. This time, though, Garfunkel's old body didn't respond as it had. After a few days, he could again walk, but the stroke had crippled his back hip. He tip-toed slowly, like an old man.

The stroke also took away what remained of his sight and hearing. We'd carry him outside for his necessaries, and he'd turn in panicked circles searching for the people who were clapping for him 2 feet away. Finally, he could no longer control himself. One evening, he limped into the kitchen, looked at Marcia and relieved himself on the floor.

She could tell he felt miserable about it. He was a prideful dog, and his look said, "Look what's happened to me."

The next day we took him in.

It was the right thing to do, but ask any dog lover and he will tell you that doesn't make it any easier.

Suddenly, there is something missing in our lives. For nights after he was gone, we would go to lay his favorite blanket out on the floor for him to sleep on, as we always did. Then we'd catch ourselves and feel sad again.

A friend who lost a dog some months ago says people don't understand why she still isn't over it. Someone actually said to her, "It was only a dog." I hope she punched him for such stupidity. Dogs are not just dogs. They become part of you.

And for my part, dogs often have better qualities than many people. Who gives you unconditional love like a dog? Who greets you at the door when you come home as if you're the greatest creature on the whole planet? Who forgives you almost instantly for anger? If people had more dog qualities, this would be a better world.

So long, Garfunkel.

May you finally catch a squirrel in heaven.

— January 9, 1995

Squirrel mania? Not so crazy

People said I was crazy. They said that because I had written several articles warning people about the increasingly aggressive nature of the squirrel population here in Flint that I was losing touch with reality.

"Get a grip on yourself," they said when I wrote that it wouldn't surprise me if the obviously steroid-crazed squirrels in my neighborhood someday tackled me as I filled the bird feeder and buried me alive in the yard like a large, hairy nut.

Even my wife was deeply concerned after that one.

"Take out the garbage," she said.

Well. Maybe not that concerned.

Still, other people acted like my train had jumped the track, which it most definitely has not. They said: "You act like the squirrels are trying to take over the world or something."

Ha ha! Squirrels taking over the world! Now THAT'S crazy! Where do people get these ideas? Squirrels aren't going to take over the world.

They're going to take over the country.

You would know this if you'd been closely monitoring the media in recent months, as I have been.

If you had, you too would have noted the huge surge in suspicious squirrel activity lately. Consider the following true news items:

• A man in Sacramento, Calif., was jailed recently for hitting his wife with a frozen squirrel. Police said the man was arguing with his wife when he stormed into the kitchen, removed the squirrel from a freezer and struck her in the head with it.

• According to an Associated Press report, a Traverse City man was forced to electrify his metal bird feeder pole to keep away marauding squirrels.

"(I'm) a little afraid of it myself," he said.

• The Flint Journal reported that 3,600 Consumers Power Co. customers lost power when a squirrel, obviously on a suicide mission, turned itself into rodent toast by attacking a substation on Judd Road, causing a fuse to blow.

• In Colorado, Gov. Roy Romer – who apparently had very little else to do that day – pardoned a squirrel dubbed "Killer T-Rex," which had been sentenced to die for repeatedly attacking visitors to Denver's Museum of Natural History. Visitors complained that T-Rex leaped onto their pant legs and sometimes bit them if they didn't give him food.

And, finally, there is the most shocking item of all: Squirrels are taking over the White House. As Dave Barry would say, I am not making this up.

This is according to Richard Mallery of Williamsburg, the publisher of the Dick E. Bird News, a monthly newspaper with a circulation of 5,000 that offers readers "a tongue in beak account of backyard bird feeding."

We use only the finest sources for this column.

Anyway, Mallery recently discovered this amazing bit of information from a faithful Dick E. Bird subscriber who forwarded a letter from (this is a real title) White House Chief Usher Gary Walters.

This subscriber, it seems, had written the White House wondering why bird feeders had been absent from the White House lawn since Ronald Reagan took office.

In his response, Chief Usher Walters indicated there were no birdhouses at the White House because the White House already suffers from a major rodent problem. (I had to bite my tongue when I heard that.)

Birdhouses, he said, would only attract more rodents, particularly squirrels, which Mallery says are already overrunning the White House grounds, according to a recent

Jack Anderson column.

So there you have it: Clear evidence of this nation's growing squirrel problem. No longer are squirrels content to simply beg for bread crumbs in the park or, in the case of my back yard, sit up in the trees tossing vicious insults at my cat.

Instead they have graduated to naked acts of aggression, cryogenic experimentation, assault, thievery and even kamikaze-style attacks on this nation's power sources, which, any military expert will tell you, is the first step to take in any coup attempt.

Ask yourself: Is that what's happening here? Are the squirrels practicing for a final assault? Are we witnessing the first steps in a sinister squirrel plan to overthrow the government of the United States of America?

I don't know, but it wouldn't surprise me if one day the lights dim momentarily at 1600 Pennsylvania Avenue and Vice President Dan Quayle winds up buried out in the yard with the rest of the nuts.

Then we'll see who's crazy.

— February 13, 1992

Love and Marriage

Is talking key to successful marriage?

Communication is vital in a marriage. All the magazines say so. One thing they tell you is to keep talking, no matter what. Don't become like some couples and sit through entire meals without speaking. Talk. Chat. Like friends. Discuss books. Discuss movies. Discuss cracks in the wall, if you have to. Just keep talking.

Which is how I came to bring up the movie "Indecent Proposal."

This is the new one in which Robert Redford, who is playing (talk about a stretch) an extremely wealthy man, offers Demi Moore, who is married, a million dollars to sleep with him.

She does, and it ruins her marriage. But then, she's married to Woody "Cheers" Harrelson, so it's no big loss.

Everyone's talking about this movie.

A disc jockey in Detroit, for instance, asked callers if they would allow their spouses to sleep with a stranger for a cool mil.

One guy answered, "For a million, he could have my wife, my sister and my mother. For a whole damn week!"

The DJ asked if he wouldn't feel guilty or miss them.

"Hey!" he said. "With a million, I could always buy them back."

The family man lives.

Anyway, one night at the dinner table, when the conversation lagged, I asked my wife, Marcia, if she'd let me sleep with someone for a million bucks. She giggled.

"What's so funny?" I asked.

"Oh, nothing," she replied.

"No, really. What's so funny?"

"Well, if you must know, the idea of a woman paying you a million dollars to sleep with her is just, you know."

"No, I don't know. Tell me."

"It's just funny, that's all."

"It's not funny!" I said. "Plenty of women would pay to sleep with me!"

"Name one."

"Let's see. There's, um, that woman down at the ... no, not her. And there's, hmmm, no, not her either. How about ...?"

"See."

"See what?"

"You can't think of any."

"That's just because I don't know any women with a million bucks."

"Uh-huh."

"OK, fine. So maybe I'm no Robert Redford."

"That's for sure," she mumbled.

"What was that?" I said.

"Oh, nothing. You were saying?"

"Just suppose a woman, any woman, offered me a million dollars to sleep with her. Would you let me?"

"How bad off are we financially?"

"Very bad. And this is a million dollars we're talking about."

"Is this cash or check?"

"Cash."

"And are you going to roll over and fall asleep afterward, like you usually do with me? And if so, does she get a discount?"

"Very funny. Would you let me sleep with her or not?"

"Absolutely not."

"Aha! I thought so."

"I mean, I'd hate to put the poor thing through such an ordeal."

"Well, I'd survive."

"I meant her."

"Hey!"

"Now how about me?" she said.

"How about you what?" I replied.

"Would you be angry if I slept with Robert Redford for a million dollars?"

"It doesn't matter how I'd feel because it would never happen."

Her eyebrows arched.

"What do you mean it would never happen?" she asked. "Are you trying to tell me that I'm not worth a million?"

"All I meant is, it wouldn't happen because that's just the way you are."

"Oh, I get it. You're saying I'm cold!"

"No, I'm simply saying I know you, and you'd never do anything like that, even for a million dollars."

"I don't know. This IS Robert Redford we're talking about."

"What does that mean?"

"It means that most women would pay him to sleep with them. That's what's so unrealistic about the movie."

"Oh, I see. So if Robert Redbutt ..."

"Redford."

"Whatever. So you're telling me that if Robert Redford walked in here with a million dollars, you would sleep with him?"

"Actually, I'm more into Kevin Costner."

"Fine. Kevin Costner. Would you?"

"I could be persuaded."

"Fine! Then if Demi Moore walked in here and offered me a million to sleep with her, I'd do it in a second! And boy would I give her her money's worth. Why, she'd probably end up begging me to drop you and stay with her. What do you think about that?!"

At which point she giggled and left the room.

If you ask me, communication is definitely overrated.

— April 11, 1993

H-H-H-ELP! T-t-turn up the h-h-heat

To whom it may concern: Please send help. Or a space heater. I'm not sure how much longer I can hold on. It's cold. Very cold. Fingers hardly working anymore. Home keyboard hard to tap. Thoughts muddled. Please excuse.

It's my wife. She's trying to kill me again. She does this every year. She says, "No touching the thermometer until Thanksgiving." That's the legal date for truly cold weather to start, in her mind at least. So until then, she says, if I'm cold I should put on a sweater.

Which I did. But it kept getting colder and colder, and I kept putting on more and more clothes.

Now I'm wearing so many clothes I can't move. I haven't gone to the bathroom in three days. I can't waddle that far. And it wouldn't matter if I could because I'm afraid something vital might freeze and fall off if exposed to air.

I'm cold, but not that cold.

She says she is only thinking of our bank account.

But this is not a normal fall. In a normal fall, I'm burning leaves right now. Now I'm thinking about burning furniture.

It even snowed the other week. I watched it fluff down in amazement. Snow. In October. I hadn't even raked yet. I didn't know whether to rake the snow or shovel the leaves. What I do know is how badly I want to find a global warming scientist and stuff a leafy slushball down his throat.

It's getting bad. I finally told my wife the other day: Look, I must have heat, especially if you hope to have children some day.

She said: Don't be such a baby. It's not that bad.

Easy for her to say. She's never cold. The woman is a polar seal. She doesn't have blood in her veins, she has Prestone. She's always outside with no coat. She never wears a hat. She thinks January is a perfectly lovely month.

Me? I wear gloves through May. I get the chills in July. I hate the cold, even though (or maybe because) I grew up in the north, where 20 below is considered balmy.

We are as opposite as fire and ice, she and I. Come winter, I am constantly turning the thermostat up; she is constantly turning it down. Our home is either the Antarctic or Guam.

"It's freezing in here," I'll whine.

"Feels fine to me," she'll say.

"Maybe to you. Women have an extra layer of fat."

"Fat?"

"It's a biological fact."

"FAT?!"

Tip to other men in my situation: Do not bring up women's extra layer of fat, no matter what the scientists say. Believe me. It's colder in the doghouse than it is in the house.

Which brings me to the reason for this note:

If I freeze to death, it is my last request that someone bring my wife to justice. The woman can't be allowed to marry and murder again.

My suggestion: have her charged with first-degree murder. Better yet, zero-degree murder. That's how cold it feels in here.

Wait. Must stop for a moment. Left eye has frozen shut.

Ah, there. Those Bic lighters are handy. Now where was I?

Ah, yes, my wife. Not sure why she wants to kill me. Could have something to do with the laundry. I leave tissues in my pockets. She hates that.

She says: "Next time you do that, pow, zoom, straight to the moon."

See? Evidence of pre-meditation.

Or it could be the bathroom. I get hairs in the drain then forget to clean them out. She says: "Next time you do that, pal, you're dead meat."

More evidence. The woman is clearly unbalanced.

It could even be my clothes. I leave them in a pile and wait for the Clothes Fairy to pick them up.

Failing that, I wait patiently for them to hang themselves up, which they rarely do. I have lazy clothes.

All of this drives my wife nuts, so, clearly, she has motives up the wazoo for doing me in. It shouldn't be that difficult to prosecute if, in fact, she succeeds in turning me into a human Popsicle.

Of course, there will be no need for that if you send help. An extra blanket would be nice. So would a heat lamp and a copy of Playboy (my brain is cold, too).

Do what you can. And please hurry.

Thanksgiving is a long way off, and my bladder is killing me.

— *November 9, 1992*

Family flees state of our union speech

I delivered my annual state of the union address the other evening.

"Oh for crying out loud," groaned my wife, the lovely yet formidable Marcia. "Not again."

"Tut, tut," I replied. "If the president can give a State of the Union address, the least I can do is give an address on the state of our union."

She had a "union this, pal" look on her face – the same look, coincidentally enough, that Newt had on his face during most of the president's speech – but I proceeded anyway.

"Good evening and welcome," I intoned. "Before I begin, I would like to acknowledge a few people here tonight who are near and dear to my heart: my wife, Marcia, and our son, Sam. Please stand and be recognized by the audience."

"We ARE the audience," she said, rolling her eyes.

"And may I remind you," I continued, "that it is customary at these addresses to interrupt me with wild, raucous applause and catcalls of support every third sentence or so."

"You're insane," Marcia replied. "You know that, don't you?"

"Now, in general, I would have to say that the state of our union is sound."

"In general?"

"Our household economy, while not expansive, has rebounded nicely from 1994's little financial setback."

"You mean the birth of our son? I'd hardly call that a ..."

"Peace talks continued toward ending the long and bitter

dispute over whose job it is to clean the fish tank."

"Look, buster, they're your fish, so it's your ..."

"And a compromise was reached on the long-standing issue over whether it is a big, hairy federal offense to leave an occasional pair of underwear on the bedroom floor."

"Compromise? You pick it up or I throw it out. It's that sim-"

"Still, as with any union, there were a few minor problems."

"Oh, really?"

"As chief executive, I was not at all pleased to have my veto on Friday night movie rentals overridden time and time again, especially when it came to the loathsome 'The Bridges of Madison County.' "

"That was a good movie! And who ever said you were the chief executive?"

"Then, too, the Andy Bill, under which I am not to be disturbed while watching a crucial basketball game on television, was met with far less than bipartisan support."

"With you they're all crucial."

"And, frankly, a certain special interest group once again played far too large a role in influencing a key household decision-maker, namely you."

"Special interest group? You mean my mother? Listen ..."

"In closing, I would like to say that while I am very pleased with the state of our union, I think it is vital that certain people, who shall remain nameless, accept the following challenges if we are going to fulfill our destiny of greatness."

"And those would be?"

"I challenge you to curtail deficit spending so that we do not burden future generations with unreasonable debt, as we have so often in the past."

"Hey, I needed those shoes."

"I challenge you to end the deadly scourge of warming your icy cold toes on my nice warm body in bed."

"But that's why I married you."

"But most of all, I urge you to rub my back wherever and whenever I ask. Because as we all know, a relaxed back is the backbone of a strong union. Thank you and good night."

At that point, she stormed out of the room, Sam in tow.

I have a feeling I'm not going to enjoy the opposing viewpoint.

— *January 29, 1996*

Entertainment not right name for this center

If you and your spouse are looking for an activity that combines the chance to spend some quality time together with the potential that, by the end of said time, you will want to rip one another's face off, I suggest a do-it-yourself home improvement project.

My wife and I recently completed such an activity, albeit a relatively minor one, and, let me tell you, it's something we'll remember long after the divorce is finalized.

What we did is buy a "home entertainment center."

We should have known better.

First of all, to be honest with you, the name is a bald-faced lie. Because a home entertainment center doesn't actually do anything to entertain you, such as tell you jokes or anything. It just sits there looking big and expensive. The Better Business Bureau ought to hear about this.

Second, this home entertainment center was labeled "Assembly Required," which is furniture industry code for "We DARE you!"

Right there we should have walked out of the store, since the two of us are classified "functionally mechanically impaired," meaning we're pretty sure we own both a regular screwdriver and a Phillips head screwdriver, but we're not entirely sure which is which.

But we were blinded by our lust for a complete living room because ever since we married ours has been making an excruciatingly slow transformation from neo-college to Actual Adult Human Beings Live Here.

What I mean is that, in the beginning, our elegant, yet functional, interior design theme was probably best described as "early American poor."

This look consisted of plastic milk crates (bookshelves), more plastic milk crates (TV stand) and twin electric cable spools (end tables), all of it boldly highlighting the piece de resistance of our living room ensemble, a three-legged couch bummed from her sister and covered with a bedspread the color of regurgitated chocolate milk.

As you can imagine, the overall effect created by this chic look was the envy of all our just-out-of-college friends, all of whom also subscribed to the minimalist look first popularized by the Flintstones, whose only apparent furniture items were a stone easy chair and a floor lamp with a brontosaurus-skin lamp shade, both of which would magically appear in the background of every interior scene.

But as the years passed and our income grew we yearned for something different, something unique. Something, oh, nonplastic.

And so slowly we began buying things, the latest of which was the entertainment center.

We should have known right away there'd be trouble. When a 7-foot-by-5-foot-by-3-foot piece of furniture fits in a box 4 feet long and 3 inches high, alarm bells ought to go off in your brain, don't you think?

But they didn't in ours, and so we carted the thing home one evening and immediately attempted construction, which was a mistake since it was about 90 degrees inside.

This meant our patience for one another was not at what you would call an all-time high, as evidenced by the phrase, "THAT'S NOT HOW YOU DO THAT!"

This phrase was in use all night, owing to the basic genetic difference between men and women when it comes to construction projects, wherein a woman will want to proceed slowly and methodically, reading the instructions for each step, while a man's basic approach is more along the lines of "Instructions? I don't need no STINKING instructions."

This is a very guy thing to do. Guys like to pretend they know what they are doing, even when they don't.

So when a guy, for example, puts a home entertainment center door in backward, and his wife – aka Little Miss Know-It-All – alerts him to this fact by pointing out that most door handles go on the *outside*, he will carefully assess the situation, then do one of two things.

He will either say, "You sure? It looks OK to me." Or he will blame the directions, which he didn't read. (Not me, you understand. But most guys.)

Anyhow, in only the time it would take to complete a marathon crawling backward, we had that sucker together, and I must tell you, it was quite a feeling.

We were dripping with sweat, emotionally exhausted and physically drained, but we had done it! We had built ourselves a home entertainment center!

Maybe we aren't so incompetent after all, we said. Maybe we'll undertake another home improvement project someday. Maybe even next week! Hey, we've been wanting a bedroom bookcase ...

Then we noticed all these extra parts.

— August 6, 1990

Hairy subject of marriage

Today we begin a new feature called "Ask Dr. Marriage," in which we hope to provide helpful advice to men mystified by the creatures with whom they share the cohabitational experience.

We expect no shortage of questions. Our question today is: What should I do if my wife comes home with a new hairdo?

This is a very good question, one men throughout the ages have had to deal with.

For instance, from cave paintings we know that cave men would often return from the hunt and grunt for their dinners without once noticing that their wives had had the prehistoric equivalent of a new permanent.

This is one reason you don't see many cave men around these days.

So you can see that a lot is riding on what type of response you give to this important question.

The main thing you don't want to do, as we have already demonstrated, is not notice that your spouse has had something done, follicle-wise.

Women hate that. In Dr. Marriage's experience, women want men to notice any and all changes they make to their appearance.

If they change, say, from Golden Coral blush to Sunset Orchard Peach blush – two colors that are, for all practical purposes, identical – they figure we ought to notice. And you can hardly blame them, since we are the reason they fuss with their looks so much in the first place.

There are two problems with this, however.

First, women are much more advanced in the area of color identification than men. Dr. Marriage has noticed this in his own marriage. He will often say something innocent like, "That's a nice purple sweater." To which his wife will respond in a tone of voice that clearly suggests she thinks he is completely color-blind, "That's not purple, that's mauve."

Second, attention to detail is not your average man's strong suit, at least as far as fashion is concerned.

Use a hammer from his workbench and then replace it with the head facing the wrong way, and the average man will not only notice, but he will ask you why you're "messing" with his stuff.

But meet him at the door wearing nothing but Saran Wrap and he is apt to look puzzled for a moment and ask, "Something's different. Wait. Let me guess. You lost a pound!"

Whereupon his wife will deck him.

This is a problem Dr. Marriage himself had recently.

His wife, whom he would like to add at this point is a VERY lovely and EXTREMELY forgiving person, called him one day at work and said, "I have a surprise for you when you get home."

Which made Dr. Marriage think that the toilet had overflowed again, since that is usually what Mrs. Marriage means by a surprise. (Dr. Marriage has been married a long, long time. Had we mentioned that?)

But that wasn't it at all, so Dr. Marriage and his wife had the following conversation, only we have deleted the bad language:

DR. MARRIAGE: "I'm home. What's wrong with the toilet?"

MRS. MARRIAGE: "There's nothing wrong with the toilet."

DR. MARRIAGE: "So what's the surprise?"

MRS. MARRIAGE (irritated): "You mean you don't know?"

DR. MARRIAGE: "How could I know if it's a surprise?"

MRS. MARRIAGE (really irritated): "It's as plain as the nose on your face! And your nose is huge!"

DR. MARRIAGE: (nervously looking around): "Uh, you got the carpet shampooed?"

MRS. MARRIAGE (really, really irritated): "I can't believe you!"

DR. MARRIAGE: (sweat glands on full alert): "Wait! I've got it! Uh, you, um, ha ha, you ..."

MRS. MARRIAGE (attaining world class levels of irritation): "My hair! Look at my hair!"

Which Dr. Marriage then did. His wife, who has had hair down to her shoulder blades for the past seven years, had what is called a "bob."

Why they call it a "bob," Dr. Marriage doesn't know. They don't call men's haircuts "nancy," do they?

But that's a mystery for another column. The point is, a bob is pretty short. And Dr. Marriage was deeply embarrassed that he failed to notice, so he tried to remedy the situation with some enthusiasm.

Dr. Marriage: "It's nice, honey!"

Mrs. Marriage: "Nice? That's it? Nice?!"

But apparently not *enough* enthusiasm.

Dr. Marriage: "No! No! You look great! I swear!"

Mrs. Marriage: "If you really liked it you would have noticed it in the first place! How come you didn't notice!? How come you ..."

Dr. Marriage would like to tell you what the end result of this conversation was, but he is still having it.

—June 13, 1993

What should a guy call his in-laws?

Sylvia, Sylvia, Sylvia. Jim, Jim, Jim.

There. At long last I can say those words.

Not that they're awful words, mind you. They are simply the given first names of my in-laws, and for the longest time I could not bring myself to utter them.

During my courtship with my wife, how I would address her parents was not an issue. They were adults. I was not, other than in the formal post-18 sense. Courtesy titles followed by their last name seemed sufficient.

After our wedding, the issue became cloudier. Using Mr. and Mrs. suddenly seemed awfully stuffy, particularly since I had grown to know and like them.

Yet I didn't feel close enough to them that I could abruptly begin using their first names. Nor had they ever made clear their preference in the matter, though I'm certain they felt as much anxiety over it as I did.

And so for years I did exactly what many young, married people do in the same situation.

I called them nothing at all.

Zip.

Nada.

Situations requiring the use of their names were scrupulously avoided.

Introductions were the exception.

Using their first and last names during introductions didn't seem so bad, but that did me little good in other instances since I couldn't very well go around saying things like, "How are you today, Sylvia Walworth?"

Therefore, each stay at their home inevitably included a litany of awkward, comical scenes that now seem straight out of a Woody Allen film, although they were anything but funny to me at the time.

For instance, the mashed potatoes would be across the table in front of Sylvia. The gravy would be near Jim.

My mind and pulse would begin to race. How to get a combination of the two without using their names.

"Boy," I'd finally blurt to no one in particular, making eye contact with the wall. "Those potatoes *sure were great*."

Usually, they'd pick up on the hint, give me what I needed and things would be fine. Until the next time.

Why is this so hard for so many people? If my married friends are any indication, there are millions and millions of no-name in-laws out there.

Perhaps the problem is that most of us don't see our in-laws very often. When they are out of sight the problem is out of mind.

When we do see them, falling back on old ways is easier than creating new ones. We know the tune so we dance to it, the two-step of avoidance.

Or perhaps some of us will forever feel like children around our own or our spouse's parents.

My father, throughout their entire 30-odd years of marriage, called my mother's mother nothing, even when talking with his wife.

"Your mother ..." he would say to her.

Whatever the cause, the solution is not easy. Or rather, it is easy, it's just not easy to do. I finally learned this.

"What do you think they want me to call them?" I asked my wife as we pulled into her parent's driveway one weekend.

She gave me her customary response: "I don't know. Why don't you ask them?"

Yeah, right.

"How about 'Mom and Dad'?" I said.

"You tried that," she responded.

I had. Once. It sounded awful and contrived.

"Why don't you just take the plunge?" she said at last. "If

you do it once, it'll get easier after that."

I knew she was right. I'd said the same thing to her when she faced the issue with my parents, although, as usual, she had handled the event far better than I imagined I would.

Anyway, that evening, I danced my usual dance, waiting for the right moment, which finally came after dinner.

We were all sitting in the living room. I was getting up to get some more coffee. This was it. The big moment.

As nonchalantly as I could, I said, "Can I get anyone some more coffee? Marcia? Doug? ... Jim? Sylvia?"

Her parents were momentarily startled. The corners of Sylvia's mouth curled ever so slightly. Upward, thank heavens. In fact, I think it was almost a smile of relief.

Later on my wife told me how impressed she was by my performance.

"Wow," she said. "You did that so effortlessly."

Little does she know.

— November 3, 1994

Beware of simple sneeze

It started with a sneeze.

"Bless you," she said. "That's one."

I sneezed again.

"Bless you again," she said. "That's two."

I sneezed a third time, a little hiccup of a sneeze.

"There it is!" she crowed. "Sneeze No. 3. Are you aware of the fact that you have a sneeze pattern?"

"I most certainly do not!" I said.

"Yes, you do. It's always CHOO! CHOO! ... chew! Two hard sneezes, then a pause, then a little baby one."

"Well, that's better than stifling your sneezes that way you do. You're gonna blow your brains out someday."

"I only do that because it's more hygienic. At least I don't spray everyone in the room when I sneeze."

"I don't spray everyone in the room when I sneeze. I just didn't have a tissue. I guess I didn't know that the way I sneeze bothers you."

"It doesn't 'bother' me. It's just, you know."

"No, I don't 'know.' Tell me."

"It's just, I don't know, sort of a pet peeve of mine."

"Oh, I see. And do you have any other 'pet peeves' I should know about?"

"Relax, dear. Besides that one little thing, you're an absolutely perfect husband. How DID I get so lucky?"

"No, really. Is there anything else I do that irritates you?"

"Come on now, don't get upset. I was just ..."

"You can tell me! I can take it!"

"OK, if you must know, it bothers me a little when you leave used tissues in your pockets. I have to pick them out before I do the wash. It's gross."

"I see. Anything else?"

"Well, since we're on the subject, I'm not too fond of the way you put the juice pitcher back in the refrigerator when it's all but empty."

"You're enjoying this, aren't you?"

"No, it's just that ..."

"You have some irritating habits, too, you know."

"Oh, is that so?"

"Yes, that's so?" How about the way you use my hairbrush?"

"Your brush is better than mine."

"But you leave hairs all over it. Why don't you pull the stupid things out?"

"Because they make that icky sound when you tear them out. You know I can't stand that sound. Besides, at least I don't leave my whiskers in the sink, like SOMEONE I know."

"I don't leave my whiskers in the sink!"

"Well, it's either you or the sink's growing hair. Maybe we should call the exterminator."

"Very funny. But while we're on the subject of razors, maybe you'd like to tell me who's been using my razor to shave her legs?"

"The children?"

"We don't have any children."

"OK, I use it. What's the big deal?"

"The big deal is it screws up the blade, and when I shave with it I end up losing three quarts of blood!"

"You have been looking kind of pale lately."

"Har-dee-har-har. You're pretty funny for someone who refuses to replace the toilet paper roll when it's empty."

"Oh, like that's a crime?! At least I pick my dirty underwear up off the floor, unlike like some little oinker I know."

"It always comes back to the underwear, doesn't it? Did it ever occur to you that I'm saving it to pick up at the end of the week?"

"That's disgusting."

"It's not disgusting. Just efficient. Is it my fault that you pick it up after three days, thereby ruining my system?"

"What system? Your system is being a slob. What is it with men?"

"Oh, now it's a man thing."

"Yes, it's a man thing. Every woman I know says the same thing: Men are slobs. Tell me, is it some sort of gene thing?"

"No, it's not a 'gene thing.' It's just that women are obsessively neat. Men simply have neatness in perspective."

"And what perspective is that?"

"That there are more important things than cleaning."

"Such as?"

"Anything."

"I thought so."

"Say, you're pretty smug for someone whose mother calls at 7:30 in the morning every Sunday."

"And you're pretty cocky for someone who sometimes forgets to flush the toilet."

"Oh, yeah? Well, how about the way you ..."

We went on like this for a solid hour.

Today's lesson: Marriage is like a sneeze. Sometimes it's just one blow after another.

— March 29, 1993

Thoughts that go through minds of men

I was driving down the road the other day when a psychobabbler came on the radio.

Psychobabblers, in case you don't know the term, are psychologists who go on the radio and babble.

We keep things simple around here.

Anyway, this pyschobabbler was of the opinion that guys need to share their feelings more often.

Women, she said, share their innermost thoughts, feelings and emotions with other people and are therefore healthier and happier.

Men, on the other hand, tend to keep their thoughts to themselves, which isn't healthy, said the psychobabbler. Keep emotions inside of you too long and they'll start to expand, like yeast, and before you know it, you'll explode, and there will be bits of emotional bread everywhere.

I'm paraphrasing, you understand.

Most women I know would agree with this theory. They marvel at the male thought process and wonder constantly what the heck it is we're thinking about.

I know this because my wife is constantly asking me.

"What are you thinking about?" she'll ask, noticing that I have a look of intense concentration on my face, as if I'm trying to decide the best way to reduce the federal deficit or something.

I, of course, give the Standard Male Reply: "Oh, nothing."

This is her cue to go into Standard Female Response Mode, which consists of her rolling her eyes and sighing.

So what ARE we thinking about?

Well, as a public service to women everywhere, I have decided to end the mystery. Here, then, are a few typical thoughts that go through the typical guy's brain during a typical day:

I sure could use some sex right now.

Damned cat.

I hate this fiber crap. Where are the Fruit Loops?

That Kathie Lee Gifford talks too damned much. How does Frank stand it?

She sure is cute, though.

I really shouldn't eat this doughnut.

Or this doughnut.

Or this one.

Ah, what the hell.

Damn! My pants shrank again! Lousy manufacturers!

She wants me. I can tell.

Was it the Pittsburgh Steelers who won the Super Bowl back in '73?

No, wait. It was the Dolphins.

Or maybe the Redskins. That's it, the Redskins!

She said something! Quick! What'd she say! Respond! Respond!

Whew! She didn't suspect a thing.

Look at that jerk! Hey, tailgate this, you ———!

I could take him if I had to.

Ted Williams, lifetime batting average .344.

Either the sink's growing hair or I'm going bald.

Oh, god! Women hate bald! I'm doomed!

Of course Yul Brynner was bald and women liked him.

Damned kids.

Is my fly zipped?

My car's bigger than his car.

Plumber? I don't need no stinking plumber!

Here it comes. She's gonna say, "I told you we needed a plumber!"

Four more paper wads in the wastebasket and I'm the Champion of the Woooooorld!

Mom made this better.

I wonder if Madonna would sleep with me?

Boy, I sure could use some sex right now.

So there you have it, ladies. As you suspected, men do in fact have deep feelings and emotions on a wide range of topics and issues.

It's just that most of them are stupid.

— January 11, 1993

The Family

Hey, Mom, can I sit at big table?

I am 31. I have a wife, a job and maxed out credit cards. I even have car payments and a subtle, nagging feeling that my body is beginning the long, slow change from "young" to "they're not love handles, they're maturity rolls."

I say these things to point out the fact that I am an adult. In fact, I am as adult as they come. I no longer watch Saturday morning cartoons. I no longer can remember what it was that possessed me to consume the contents of Pixie Sticks. And more often than not I excuse myself when I burp.

Hell, I don't even get carded anymore when I buy beer. And teen-agers, the little brats, tend to call me "Sir" or "Mister," which always causes me to whirl and look for my dad.

Adult, adult, adult. It's written all over me.

So why, I want to know, do I always get stuck at the kids' table at Thanksgiving and Christmas?

That's a rhetorical question. I know why I and a million other baby boomers end up at the kids' table. It's because our families are too damned big. It's always been that way.

The older adults – the assorted moms, dads, uncles, grandparents, older children – still get the big table, where all the good stuff starts out: the turkey, the mashed potatoes, the stuffing etc.

And we kids, the surplus people, no matter if we have pot bellies, PhDs and 15 percent balloon mortgages, still end up at the rickety little card table in the other room, staring at the damned relish tray and a dish of creamed corn.

Children of the Creamed Corn. That's what they should call us.

We are the ones who wait impatiently for the big table to fork over the main courses, the ones who always get the dark meat, the cold mashed potatoes, the empty gravy boat.

We are the ones who eat in silence because we're too busy wondering what the hell everyone is laughing about in the next room. (These people never seem to have that much fun when WE dine with them).

We are the ones whose table has the hard chairs, the paper napkins, the Disney glasses, the stained tablecloth and that damned porcelain turkey centerpiece Mom's had since the Eisenhower administration.

We are the ones who are always asked, "Is everything OK in there?" when the answer is ridiculously obvious.

And, finally, we are the ones who have to sit with the real kids, who remind us, in no uncertain terms, why our parents were so happy to have us at a separate table in the first place all those years.

Some of you big-table people are laughing. You're saying: "What's the big deal? If there were room, we'd let you sit with us. But there isn't room, so you can't. Besides, the kids' table can't be that bad, right?" To which we mature, rational kid-tablers respectfully say: THEN WHY DON'T YOU SIT THERE?! HUH?!

Because it *is* that bad. I don't care who you are, sitting at the kids' table makes you feel like a kid. It's undignified.

Bill Clinton's a baby boomer, but I'll bet his mommy doesn't make him sit at the kids' table anymore. So why should we? We're adults, too.

At what point do we get our turn? Is it always going to be a seniority thing, like everything else in our lives? Do we have to wait until somebody dies to get our shot? Huh?

Let's hope not. We're all adults here. We should be able to work out an adult solution. If not, there could be trouble.

Children of the Creamed Corn, rise up! Demand your place at the adult table of life!

Remember: You have nothing to lose but your cold potatoes.

— *November 10, 1990*

When parents decide to go separate ways

I wasn't going to write about this, but it hurts, and writing has always been a soothing balm, so I will.

It's my parents.

They're divorcing.

Or at least it's very likely that they will. The date is set for later this month. But if it is happening to your parents, even if you're an adult, you never give up the awful, desperate, childlike hope that it won't.

It started with the toast. My father suddenly stood during the family Thanksgiving meal, raised his glass and spoke in a voice heavy with emotion of how much we mean to him.

He is normally an emotionally reserved man, so the announcement touched and troubled us. I could see as much in the eyes of my sister and four brothers. Several of us exchanged quick, apprehensive glances.

My father's eyes, on the other hand, for the length of a breath, seemed like the lenses of twin cameras, soaking us in, capturing us, storing every last detail of a family, his family, at holiday.

As it turns out, his was the bittersweet declaration of a man who suspects things might never again be the same. A few weeks later, shortly before Christmas, my mother, her voice low and trembling, phoned with the news.

"You're kidding?" I said, laughing nervously, although I could tell she wasn't.

In the months since, we, the grown children of a union that lasted just long enough for the youngest to enter college, have experienced something akin to the stages of mourning that the living go through when someone dies. (And something has died, hasn't it?)

At first, there was disbelief. To be sure, I didn't believe it. I acted remarkably normal for a few days following the call, or so my wife tells me, although I do remember sitting for a long time before our Christmas tree, squinting my eyes to make the bulbs fuzzy, allowing the phantasmagoric blur to draw me in and comfort me, the way it did when I was a child.

Then came anger and guilt. What's wrong with them? What's wrong with us? How could we have not known? (But, then, how, could we have known?) Could we have helped? Why didn't they tell us something was wrong? There were hints, weren't there? Of course there were. But what difference does it make now?

Divorce generates nothing so much as unanswerable questions.

Then came a wild, desperate feeling of unconnectedness, of a safety net suddenly disappearing. Supposedly, we children, by now, are adept enough at walking life's high wire that this should not frighten us. But, at least in my case, I was suddenly terrified to look down.

After all, what can you count on if not your parents being together, being "there"? What's your base? And while we're at it, where the heck are we going to gather for Christmas each year?

And now, finally, there is at least some grudging sense of acceptance. Barring a last-minute reconciliation, it will become final this month, on a date roughly equidistant between Mother's Day and Father's Day.

The irony therein is not lost on me.

And my parents?

They're doing fine. Or at least as fine as two people can be who are rending the fabric of an existence they've known and sought comfort in almost since they were children. No matter the division of property, there are no winners in divorce.

When we talk on the phone, which we do more often than we used to, I tell each of my parents that I love them, that I am behind them and so on. I assume my siblings do the same.

What else can you say? This kind of wound is healed by no other poultice but time. So we do the best we can. When they are sad, we console. When they are bitter, we commiserate. When they are angry, we try not to judge. (Already we are learning the curious dance of not choosing sides.)

Most of all, we listen and try to understand. For, like us, they are out there on that long, thin strand, suddenly without a net, and they, too, probably worry about what will catch them if they fall.

More and more I think I know the answer. Because more and more I sense that little has truly changed, that perhaps things are only ... different.

We are still their net; they are still ours, albeit separately. Divorce can change many things, but maybe it cannot change everything.

And maybe we'll all be all right. As long as we don't look down.

— May 10, 1990

A houseful of memories on the block

Somehow it seems there should be more to it than this. I don't know. A ceremony. A few words. Something.

But standing here with my wife in the snow in the driveway of my family's house in the Upper Peninsula, I can't think of anything to do or say that doesn't seem stupid or mawkish. Besides, I just don't feel like it.

So I snap a photo of Marcia standing in front of it, like it's the Lincoln Memorial or something.

Then she says, "Let me take one of you." I shrug, shuffle into place. She'll snap a picture and that will be it.

Farewell, childhood home, I knew thee well. And I shall know thee no more.

It's been coming for months now, ever since my parents divorced last May after more than 30 years of marriage.

The house where I'd grown up, where the eight of us – my mother, my father, me, my four brothers and my sister – lived since I was in the sixth grade, was suddenly too big and too expensive for my father tc manage alone. So he decided to let the bank take it. It was the only logical thing to do.

The bank wasted little time. They planted a "For Sale" sign in the front yard almost immediately and told my father he'd have to be out by the middle of this month.

I think probably the sign embarrasses him. He's like that. Very proud. I doubt he can bring himself to look at it. I know

I can't.

It was hard enough just staying here at the house over Christmas. But I knew this would be my last chance, so I did.

My brothers decided not to. Perhaps it was too painful. Or perhaps they're not as sentimental as I am. I'm awful that way.

Whatever. My father seemed to appreciate my presence, even though he didn't say so. I could tell because he cleaned up. My sister, the only one of us kids left in town now, told me that after my mother moved out, he let the place go a bit. Books and magazines everywhere. Laundry on the dining room table. Nothing in the refrigerator.

None of that now. Things are ship-shape. He even built a fire in the fireplace the other night. "Haven't done this in a year," he said, smiling.

I guess he felt we brought a little life to the place. Funny. All week I felt as if something was dying.

Isn't that strange? I haven't lived in this house for 10 years, yet the thought of it not being here saddens me beyond belief. There's something about the house in which you grow up. It's the tether to which many of your memories are tied.

I walked around all week looking at things. Dumb things. My father's den, heaped as always with books and papers. A painting of a country scene that has hung in the same spot in the dining room forever. The model airplanes I made that still hang, as if in flight, from the basement ceiling. The back yard where we tumbled and played.

Everything sparked a memory. Maybe that's what upsets me the most. I cannot recall these things on my own. So with the house dies a part of my childhood, and I am left with this awful sense of time's passing.

The past is fading. The future suddenly looms larger than it seemed to yesterday, and there's nothing I can do about it.

Which is why, as I stand in the driveway, my wife of seven years pointing a camera at me, the house in the background, I can't help but feel like a lost little boy.

"Smile," she urges.

I don't smile. I raise my hand as if to wave goodbye.

It's all I can think of to do.

— January 7, 1991

Hard choices, doubts and nursing homes

e are walking into the nursing home, my family and I. We are nervous. We are here to see my grandmother who is 89. She has been here a week, and the big question is how well she likes it.

None of us is saying so, but we're afraid that if she hates the place the guilt will overwhelm us. No one wants to put a loved one into a nursing home, no matter how nice it is.

But it had to be done. For her own good. We all agreed. Unfortunately, that doesn't make it any easier.

She'd lived alone since Jan. 28, 1967, the day her husband died, and she'd always done just fine, except for the fact that there was a hole in her heart.

"Someday soon I'll be joining Scottie," she said to me a million times over the years, each time with more longing in her voice.

But she never did join him. Her body remained amazingly sound. It was her mind and spirit that eventually began slipping.

It got scary last month. She left a kettle boiling on the stove in her apartment and forgot about it. Maintenance workers noticed a burning smell, entered the apartment and threw the kettle out in the snow.

As it turns out, it was a warning. The strokes came within a week.

They didn't harm her physically, but sometimes when she spoke to you she suddenly wasn't there anymore. She was packing for a vacation to Florida with long-dead friends. She was back in an apartment in the Upper Peninsula where she used to live. Sometimes she'd even fail to recognize my mother, whose name is Christine.

"Tell Chris to visit me, dear," she'd say to my mom. "Tell Chris to visit."

The doctors said it wasn't going to change. The strokes and old age had finally caught up with her.

My mom called everyone in the family and asked what we thought she should do. The choice was both easy and impossibly hard. She wasn't sick enough for the hospital, but she couldn't live alone anymore. She needs constant care and supervision, more than any of us can provide. She needs people around to stimulate her.

She needs a nursing home.

We all agreed.

We are in my grandmother's room. Me, my mother, my wife, my sister-in-law and her young daughter. Grandma is in a chair next to the bed, which, I notice, has guardrails. A curtain splits the room in half. Behind it is a woman who, we understand, never gets out of bed, never makes a sound.

"I think she's quite elderly, dear," my grandmother whispers.

We all laugh. She looks small and frail, but she is chatting and happy to see us. She doesn't seem to notice that she's no longer in her apartment.

Across the hall, a woman moans over and over again, "Please, Lord, help me. Please, Lord, help me."

Grandma doesn't seem to notice this either. She's busy telling stories about her Scottie. She seems as normal as ever. I'm sure my mom is thinking the same thing I am: Oh, God, is this the right thing for her? Maybe we made a mistake.

Finally, we ask my grandmother how things are. How does she feel about staying here? Does she like having people around all the time? What about the meals and the nurses?

She says: "Oh, very nice, dear."

She seems to mean it, but we can't tell. Doubt is the worst thing about nursing homes.

We're in a recreation room down the hall, saying our

goodbyes. Grandma doesn't seem to notice the man who is grumbling at unseen enemies. Nor does she seem to notice the woman who pleads with passing nurses to untie the sheet that holds her to her wheelchair. But we notice.

We talk to cover our nervousness. Soon the discussion turns to the piano over against the wall. Grandma used to live in a senior citizen high-rise. She loved it there. She would play piano at social functions.

We say: Play something for us, grandma. She says: Oh, no, I couldn't. But we coax her, and she shuffles over to the piano.

She is playing an old song, "Annie Laurie," without any music, her 90-year-old hands dancing like a child's feet over the keys. She seems lost in it. And when she finishes, she is clearly delighted.

"I haven't played in years," she says, almost surprised.

The rest of us are near tears.

I say: You ought to play for the people who live here. They'd probably like that.

She says: Maybc I will, dear. Maybe I will.

— March 14, 1993

One thing can't be said too often

This is how today's phone call will go:

"Hiya, dad," I'll say. "Happy Father's Day. Howya doing?"

"Thanks," he'll reply. "Doing fine."

Then he'll chuckle that low, shy chuckle of his, as if he's embarrassed to have someone wonder how he is.

We'll talk for a minute about the Detroit Tigers – he's not a big Sparky Anderson fan. We'll talk about how his softball team is doing – at 54 he's still playing competitive slow-pitch. And we'll talk about the upcoming airplane show in Oshkosh, Wis., the one we would always attend together when I was a kid.

Then, as always, there will be a short, awkward silence followed by his familiar, "Just a minute, let me get your mother." Then I'll fumble and try to sneak in a quick "love ya" as he's tailing away from the phone like a biplane doing a barrel roll.

Often I know he's out of earshot when I say that because he doesn't respond. Other times I know I've scored a direct hit because I can hear that low, embarrassed chuckle.

Occasionally, hc'll follow that with a quiet, almost mumbled, "Love you, too," in return.

Those are the moments I cherish most.

You see, like many fathers and sons, it's always been difficult for us to express feelings to one another.

In our conversations, we've traditionally stuck to safe topics like baseball, jobs, politics. In a weird, unacknowledged way, our conversations always have been structured to avoid other areas. I suppose it's the whole silly, macho tradition that stifles us, the same John Wayne-ish tradition that says it's wrong for males in our society to embrace or cry.

Some people are puzzled when I tell them this. But to me it's just how it's always been for my father and his five sons. I suspect the same was true between my dad and his father, although I've never asked him about it. It's not something he has planned or is particularly proud of. Nor am I.

But for several years now, we've been getting better. Slowly. And in a way that will sound familiar to many people.

In the winter of 1981, my father underwent an emergency quadruple heart bypass operation. Males in our family always have been prone to heart troubles.

I was in college at the time, at Central Michigan University. My mother's voice on the other end of the phone was a scared, almost inaudible whisper, as she tried to explain that her husband, my father, was in the hospital.

I remember driving nine hours straight to reach the hospital in Green Bay, Wis., where they had taken him from our home in the Upper Peninsula.

Everyone has moments that are indelibly burned into their mind as the worst of their lives.

Mine was walking into that hospital room and seeing this active man all wan and pale in his bed, just out of surgery, with more wires attached to him than a new Chevrolet motor.

That day was the first time since childhood I told him flat out that I loved him.

Since then, we've both made efforts to communicate better. Many times, though, we slip back into our old patterns and talk about surface things.

I was thinking about this the other day when a song by Dan Fogelberg came on the radio.

It's called "The Leader of the Band." It's a tribute to his father and a lament of stifled father-son relationships.

The line that hits hardest is the last. It goes: "And, Papa, I don't think I've said 'I love you' near enough."

Maybe when I call my dad today I'll say much the same thing.

— June 21, 1992

Dad batted 1.000 with us

It may sound like a cliche, but my father died the way he would have wanted to die, having just pitched in a softball game.

Softball was the world to him. He was 60 and had played for nearly 35 years, never missing a season until last summer, when, for some reason, no one asked him to play.

It nearly broke his heart. I could hear it in his voice on the phone. He didn't say so, but I knew he took not playing to mean that he was old and washed up, that a special part of his life was ending.

So, this year, when one of the best teams in town said they once again needed him – what wonderful words – he oiled up his glove and prepared for another long season.

Lord, that made him happy. He felt proud, excited. And young. I could hear that in his voice, too.

And this wasn't church league softball. This was tough stuff, a Class A league full of young spitfires fresh out of the high school jock mill, and older, shop-working giants who could smack the ball a country mile.

But the Big Fig (our nickname for him, given his middle name of Newton) pitched them tough to the end.

From what I understand, he came into what was to be his final game on this planet as a relief pitcher and quieted the opposition's bats, which had been booming all evening. He was thrilled.

Afterward, he went with his girlfriend to a nearby A&W to celebrate with a root beer float, and that's where the heart attack, the old family bugaboo, got him.

He'd been expecting it, dreading it, for years. In a way, we all had. This is a man whose father's heart had seized up, and who himself had had a bypass operation, a stroke and artery surgery, all within the last dozen years.

It drove me crazy that he continued to play. I kept picturing a line drive slamming into his scarred chest, and when he slid into second I'd cringe and nearly weep with relief when he got back up and dusted himself off.

So when the big one came, it was hardly a surprise. And, mercifully, since this is a man to whom a hospital bed was a bed of nails, he was gone within minutes.

His last regret, which he shared with my sister before he left the ballpark: that he hadn't gotten a base hit in his only time up to bat.

I chuckle when I think of that. That was my dad to a T. Never satisfied. Restless. Searching. Always wanting more.

It's a trait he passed on to his six kids, and, accordingly, we've asked ourselves over and over again: Why not more time? Why him? Why now? And we have asked these things angrily. My eldest brother, for instance, spent one of the nights before the funeral beating a pillow senseless in his hotel room.

My dad, after all, was a man who had finally gotten things together after a rough few years. He'd divorced, lost his job, suffered a stroke, gone through a major depression. Even his favorite hunting dog had died, and there's no lower blow than that.

Then, about a year and a half ago, things changed. He seemed to come out of it. He seemed like his old self, only better. Gone was the rage and anger that had always simmered just below the surface, like an underground peat fire. In its place there was acceptance, of his life and circumstances.

Simply put, he got on with things. He found a new love, rekindled his passion for airplanes, volunteered his time at the YMCA, announced at horse shows. He was even planning to help run a children's T-ball league.

I smile at the thought of it: My dad, the guy who would

always yell, "You're not trying!" when he was teaching us to catch, working patiently with kids who run to third base first.

As I said, he'd changed. And I haven't even told you about the change that meant the most to him: He'd begun expressing himself to people.

This is an amazing and wonderful thing because, like a lot of men, he couldn't do it early on in his life. I think I heard him say he loved me once or twice my entire childhood.

Eventually, it came to bother him. A few years ago he wrote me a long letter that he ended by saying: "All I have been trying to say is that I love you more than I have ever shown."

It came easier to him after that. In his last years, he laughed easier, cried harder and shared more of his feelings, good and bad, with his family than he had ever done before.

I respect the hell out of him for that. We all have challenges in life. His toughest – anyone's toughest, I suppose – was overcoming himself, and he did that.

I try to keep that in mind when I start cursing the Lord for taking him so soon. I try to remember that my dad had 60 good years, a long marriage and people around him he loved very, very much, and that, by the end, he was able to tell them so.

He was lucky in many ways. God let him go the way he would have wanted to go – quickly, without pain and following a softball game.

Now if only He'd have let him get that last base hit.

— June 24, 1993

Still connected to my father's phone number

You go through a lot of stages when someone close to you dies. There's the grief stage, the anger stage, the denial stage.

And then there's the telephone stage. That's the stage you go through when you have to disconnect the phone number your family has had for years.

I did that the other day, a few weeks after my father died, and it still hurts like hell.

The number was (906) 786-0702.

I forget a lot of things. I'm that type. I can't for the life of me remember my Social Security number. I can only remember my zip code when I don't need it. And half the time – because I never call myself, I suppose – I have trouble remembering my own phone number.

But I will never forget that number.

It was the number my family had when I was a skinny 7-year-old and we were living on 18th Avenue S. in my hometown of Escanaba. It was the number we had when we moved to 24th Avenue S. a few years later.

And it was the number I dialed when I talked to my dad last month, just a week before the heart attack got him.

By that time, he was renting the downstairs of a house in another part of town. Dad moved around town a lot after the divorce, but the phone number always moved with him. It followed him around like a loyal dog, and we always knew without thinking where we could reach him.

And now it's gone.

It's funny how much a silly thing like that can mean to you.

We even kept the phone hooked up for three or four weeks following the funeral. We didn't really need it, but no one had the heart to disconnect it.

At one point, the phone rang and we didn't answer before the answering machine clicked on.

Suddenly, there was my dad's voice.

"This is Joe. I'm not in right now ..."

It took me 10 minutes to breathe again after that.

I guess what bothers me is the obvious. If that phone number no longer exists, it means he doesn't either. He's really, truly gone. No more phone number, no more phone calls, no more father.

It's the same hollow feeling we had going through his things.

Everywhere we looked, we saw a piece of him. In his size 13½ shoes, in his half-used bottles of Old Spice, even in the clock radio, complete with 8-track player, he kept on his bed stand for longer than I can remember.

It's on my bed stand now. It's old and beat up and I don't even know if they make 8-tracks anymore, but I wouldn't give it up for the world.

That's the thing about the belongings of someone who has passed on.

Everything reeks with significance.

You don't want to throw out anything.

You want to hang onto it all.

My brother, for instance, came across a "cap buddy" in my dad's apartment. A cap buddy is a plastic mold over which you place a dirty baseball cap, which you then stick in the dishwasher.

My dad ordered that kind of stuff. He loved gadgets.

My brother kept it.

"Only dad would order one of these," he said, and we all laughed.

Keeping such things is denial. I know that. My brother knows that. You can't keep it all. Life doesn't work that way. Fathers die. Dogs get old. Old family phone numbers get passed on.

Still, it's hard to think of anyone else having certain things. I drive past the old house even now and I see other people's belongings through the windows and an unfamiliar car in the garage and I still think, "Who the heck do they think they are? That's OUR house." I want them arrested for trespassing or at least for criminal taste in furniture.

It's the same way with our phone number. I figure no one else should ever have it. That's the number I dialed when I needed a quick fix of cash at college. It's the number the police called when I was caught pegging apples. It's the number I wish I was able to call right now so I could tell my dad that he's going to be a grandfather again.

A friend just suggested that maybe what the phone company should do is allow you to retire old phone numbers, the way baseball teams retire uniform numbers. I like that idea.

(906) 786-0702.

No matter what the phone company says, it'll always be ours.

— July 26, 1993

A Rose plucked from our midst

She was born in a Southern town that no longer exists and she had red hair.

Her father was a barber and her mother was a housewife named Minnie. She was named Harriet, although everyone called her Rose, which was her middle name and a pretty fine description of her personality – sweet yet thorny.

As a girl growing up in South Carolina she once witnessed a Klan rally, where, for whatever reason, she found herself studying the Klansmen's shoes.

A few days later she was at some public function with her father.

"Daddy!" she said loudly, spotting a familiar pair of boots. "That man was under the sheet!"

She finished high school, but she never went to college because that's not what Southern women did back then, although she always wished she had.

Instead she married a man who went north to work as an engineer at the great auto plants in Flint and eventually had a hole cut in his throat after too many years of smoking.

They had a son and the doctors said it was a miracle child because she had only one ovary. In place of her other ovary was a lump that turned out to be Rose's own long-ago undeveloped twin.

The son grew up in Flint, met a woman whom neighbors

described as "a beautiful princess" and married. Perhaps owing to the fact that they were both only-children, this couple had six kids of their own, including the one with the broken heart who is writing about his grandmother today.

Rose died last week. She was 84. Hers was one of those deaths for which one is almost glad. She was simply not the same the last year of her life. No spit, no fire. Not after my father, her only son, died last June. It broke her spirit. She'd mumble over and over, "I can't believe he's gone."

At that time, she was living in a senior citizen high-rise in Escanaba, my hometown in the Upper Peninsula. With her husband long since gone, she moved there in the mid-'70s to be near her family.

The grandkids, grown up and itchy, started leaving soon thereafter. College. Jobs. Elsewhere. Eventually, only my father and my sister remained.

And when he died, she slipped fast. The high-rise managers wanted her out. She's too dangerous, they said. Even before my father's death, Rose's mind had retreated on her, and she would burn holes in her clothes and the carpet with forgotten-about cigarettes.

We moved her to an adult foster care home in a nearby town. She loved it, they loved her, as everyone always did. She was like that. But the owners soon said she'd have to go – careless smoking, night-time wandering and her famous flashing temper. Too much trouble, they said.

We moved her downstate to Mount Pleasant, where much of the family had settled and where we'd found another nice home for her. The first night there, she fell and broke her hip. Thereafter, she was in the hospital, then an adjoining long-term care facility where she would moan when the aides would try to help her walk again. "Please, please, please," she would plead in pain.

She stopped recognizing people. She could only remember long-ago events. And then, a few months ago, she all but stopped smoking, something she'd done since age 13.

In a way, we knew it was coming. And after it did, the minister said we should remember not her last few months of pain, but her years of happiness and our fond memories of her. So that's what we are doing.

We are laughing once again about her Beretta pistol. She

brought it with her to the peaceful Upper Peninsula from her town in Dixie, which had crime, and slept with it under her pillow. Pistol-packing granny, we called her: Do not disturb while sleeping.

We are remembering long-ago Wiffle ball games with her. We are remembering the summers she took care of us. We are remembering the way she'd smile and tell us to "go to the first four letters of your last name" whenever we'd tease her about the North whipping the South during the Civil War.

And I, personally, am thinking about how tickled she was whenever I'd send her anything I wrote. No matter how awful it was, she'd always beam with delight and say I was going to be the next Lewis Grizzard, who was her favorite.

But most of all I'm remembering her spunk. She had it in spades. What came into her mind, came out her mouth. "Hoof-in-mouth disease," she called it. And it's a disease she passed onto her grandkids. We, too, speak our minds.

Here's what's on my mind lately:

My dear, sweet Rose, I have absolutely no doubt whatsoever that you have not gone to the first four letters of your last name. You are in a far, far better place.

Say hi to Dad for me.

— May 2, 1994

Ghosts no longer haunt my thoughts

The ghosts are everywhere lately. In the basement. In my desk. In the closet. In my mind.

To my surprise, this is no longer a bad thing.

In fact, I welcome them.

Most recently, I found one in, of all places, the minivan. Needing room to haul some topsoil, I removed one of the bench seats. Underneath was a tumbleweed of gray fur.

Garfunkel.

Garfunkel is our dog. Was our dog. We had him put down just after Christmas, and yet it still seems odd using the past tense in reference to him, maybe because to Marcia and me he isn't past tense.

He lives on in our habits and behaviors. I come to bed in the dark at night, and still I unconsciously tiptoe around the small rug where he slept, not wanting to step on a paw. And Marcia, her first thought upon waking, before the cobwebs have cleared, is often about whether the dog needs out.

Then there is my grandmother, my sweet, thorny Rose. Digging for quarters in a change dish recently, I unearthed her watch, a slender silver thing with a broken band I'd meant to have repaired.

She passed on before I could return it to her. She willed herself away one night, I'm convinced, because her only son, my father, had died suddenly a year before and she simply couldn't bear the pain any longer.

Two weeks before she died, she told me: "It's the worst thing that can happen to you, to outlive your children."

And I believe that it is. I truly do.

My dad. Good lord. One evening I heard this beeping, and I searched and searched for it, the tiny sound driving me crazy. Finally, in an old bread box I use for storing papers I found it: my dad's black sports watch, jostled by a shifting something, come to life, two years after he last wore it.

My heart nearly stopped.

Ghosts.

They used to scare me. I would come across one of Dad's T-shirts or Garfunkel's collar or the legal papers that said I was now in charge of my grandma's care and the scab would come off my emotions and I would bleed with grief again for days.

Oh, sweet innocence. For the first 32 years of my life, I didn't know death. Death was something that happened on TV to other people elsewhere.

Then boom, boom, boom. Two years, two people and a dog I loved all gone.

Death took up what seemed like permanent residence in my home and heart, and try as I might I couldn't evict that sucker.

I read books on "dealing with death," which didn't help. All that talk about death only reminded me of what I was trying to forget in the first place.

I "shared my feelings," which is what all the psychobabblers and self-help books tell you to do.

Again, this was of no long-term help. I shared my feelings until people were sick of listening, and I would feel better momentarily.

But each night, as I lay my head on my pillow, there would be death again, clanging its chains and haunting my thoughts.

This went on until just recently, when one spring morning, I awoke and the sun was shining brightly.

I stepped out on my porch, breathed in a gush of lilac-scented air, and all of a sudden I noticed something was missing.

The pain. It was gone.

Time. It's the only cure.

It was for me, anyway. Death has at long last moved out of my house, and I couldn't be more relieved.

Now when I come across something that used to belong to my dad, my dog or my grandmother, I can and do smile. Their possessions no longer remind me that they are gone. They remind me that they once were here.

And that I had the privilege of knowing them.

— *May 21, 1995*

Fore!

Golf 'lite' just a divot in real life

For years I have watched professional golf on television. And for years something about it has bothered me, but I could never put my finger on what.

Then yesterday, having just returned from my local golf course, where I consigned the usual half dozen balls to watery graves, I settled grumpily into my chair, beer in hand, and tuned in the Buick Open in Grand Blanc Township.

As I watched the golfers hit one incredible shot after another on a course as meticulously trimmed as a Marine's hair, it suddenly occurred to me that what I was viewing was not real golf.

In real golf (i.e. golf the way most of us play it) players do not hit one incredible shot after another. Real golfers are lucky to hit one good shot per round, and the goal is not so much amassing as few strokes as possible as it is making it through 18 holes without wrapping a 9-iron around a tree or tossing one's clubs in a creek.

Nor do real golfers play on manicured courses. Real golfers play on courses that could charitably be described as scruffy.

I once played on a course in such bad shape that the divots had divots. On this course, you didn't enter the rough, which was taller than corn, without a rope tied around your waist so that your buddies could pull you back in case they heard screams.

I also once played on a course in Florida where they

warned you about – with God as my witness – alligators.

"There's a big'un on 7," the kid at the counter told us. "Suns hisself just behind the teebox. Don't worry, though, he won't bother ya."

Then he grinned and added, "Less'en he's hongry."

Hongry? Hey. Let's see Nick Faldo hit a straight drive when he's worrying about becoming lunch.

That's what I mean about the difference between real golf and PGA-style golf (hereafter referred to as "golf lite") They are completely different games. Real golf, I think, is tougher.

In golf lite, for instance, a player will fly into a tizzy if someone so much as sniffles during his backswing.

In real golf, it is customary for one golfer to talk, break wind, belch, jingle change, issue insults and offer loud, insincere advice to a fellow golfer during his backswing, particularly if there is a bet on the round.

In golf lite, players hit a shot, proceed directly to where it has landed and immediately hit the next shot.

In real golf, you wait 20 minutes while the golfers in the group ahead of you line up putts, take 47 practice swings, talk business, take mulligans, search for lost balls and scratch. Then you wait for your blood pressure to return to normal. Then you hit.

In golf lite, the average round lasts three hours or so.

In real golf, the average round can last longer than the McKinley administration. Remember the scene in "Caddyshack" where the extremely old couple would hit each ball a maximum of 15 yards? There are millions of golfers like that on your average course, and I've played behind every one of them.

In golf lite, someone else carries your clubs.

In real golf there are no caddies. You carry your own clubs (unless you're a wuss and use an electric golf cart) and by the 18th hole your left shoulder is 4 inches lower than your right.

(Real golfers wouldn't use caddies even if they could afford them, as the presence of a caddie would inhibit the employment of the real golfer's most effective scoring tools and methods – the foot wedge, the mulligan, the miraculously found ball, the suddenly improved lie and, of course, the eraser.)

In golf lite, the golfers sip Gatorade brought to them by a

flunkie.

In real golf, the golfers drink beer that they keep cold by stuffing ice into the long pocket on the side of their bag. If Greg Norman can hit par (or even the ball) after three or four Buds, then I'll think he's a great golfer.

In golf lite, play is suspended during inclement weather.

In real golf, short of a hurricane or notification that your wife is dilated to 7 centimeters, you never quit once you're on the course because you never know if the clubhouse attendant will give you your money back.

And lightning? Lightning scares the tan off of lite golfers. But real golfers know that all one has to do to protect oneself from lightning is to take out a 2-iron and hold it boldly aloft.

For real golfers know, with a certainty born of experience, that not even God Almighty can hit a 2-iron.

— August 7, 1994

Golf's secrets *never* clear to the guys

Some may scoff at O.J. Simpson's latest alibi about being out in the back yard working on his golf swing at the time of the murders of which he is accused.

But I don't. And I doubt many golfers do. In fact, to golfers this may well be the first O.J. alibi that rings true.

A swing that is true and pure is the Holy Grail of most golfers. In search of this swing, we will move heaven and earth. (As opposed to when we're on the course and not swinging well. Then we move just earth.)

O.J. said he was chipping balls into a sandbox at 10 p.m.

So? To golfers, such behavior is not unusual in the least. Once, for instance, my wife awoke at 3 in the morning to the following string of sounds: Click, clunk, "(expletive)!"

Apparently, I was sleep-putting in the living room. The click was my putter striking the ball, the clunk was the ball striking the rim of the tumbler into which I was attempting to putt, and the rest is self-explanatory.

Incidentally, my wife swears that story is true. I can't be sure. I was asleep at the time.

I also once knew a man whose wife became so upset at the amount of time he spent golfing that she marched into the living room one night holding his golf bag. "It's either me or these clubs," she fumed. "You choose."

My friend, of course, did the only thing he could do given so clear a choice, but he gets wistful remembering it.

"I really miss her sometimes," he says.

There is no doubting that men can be zealous about the game. And I say men because most women I know view golf, sensibly so, as just a game, whereas grown men will not think twice about loudly coughing up a vital organ during an opponent's backswing when there's a $30 skins at stake.

Men view golf as a religion. And we practice this religion religiously, which is why you hear so much praying around the putting green.

I have seen men practice their putting in the aisles of airplanes. I have seen them pay thousands of dollars to go on a romantic cruise with a woman, only to spend their time driving golf balls off the fantail into the ocean. (I myself, wouldn't do this. I hook so badly my shot would probably miss the ocean, boomerang around to the boat and clunk Kathie Lee Gifford on the forehead. Not that this would be a bad thing, you understand, but it would be rude.)

Male golfers have even been known to watch golf on TV. Is any more proof needed that we are insane? Golf is the single dullest thing you can see on TV besides a Cher infomercial or Willard Scott. Even golfers will tell you that. There is nothing exciting about a ball going up, a ball coming down and a geek in the crowd shouting, "You duh man!"

But we watch because we are seeking "the secret."

Plus, we are awed by anyone who can do it, who can play the damnable game of golf with any modicum of success.

Which reminds me of a story: A man brings his pet gorilla to his golf club and bets a fellow member $100 that his primate can beat him on the first hole. The member accepts, so the gorilla addresses the ball, swings and sends it on a 275-yard flight, landing on the green a foot from the pin. The man's friend concedes defeat, hands over the money and says, "That's amazing. I would love to drive the ball that well. But tell me, how does he do on a putt?"

To which the man replies, "Same as on his drives. About 275 yards."

So is O.J.'s seemingly incredible defense plausible?

Does a bear chip in the woods?

— February 6, 1995

Don't hack at presidential golfing traits

Nongolfers had themselves a good laugh at the Three Stooges last week, otherwise known as Bill Clinton, George Bush and Gerald Ford.

They played in the Bob Hope Desert Classic along with Hope and defending champ Scott Hoch, and it was not pretty. Bush hit two spectators with wayward shots, breaking at least one nose; Ford bloodied one onlooker; and Clinton's shots were repeatedly and seemingly inexorably drawn to sand traps and neighboring back yards.

How ugly was it? Fans took to calling out "incoming!" instead of the traditional "fore!" Squirrels were spotted wearing helmets. Spectators said they hadn't seen such horrifying hacking since "Friday the 13th: Part IV."

This was all widely reported, of course, which gave my nongolfing friends a lot of ammunition. "From what I hear," one said, "they make even you look good." Har har.

I'll have them know – and the rest of you scoffers out there too – that there is nothing tougher in the world of amateur sports than hitting a true golf shot when a group of strangers is watching. Nothing. Every golfer knows this. The hardest shot in golf is not a 40-foot downhill putt but the dreaded clubhouse shot. This is when you are on the first or 10th tee and everyone is watching and waiting for you to do something entertainingly awful: the club pro, the starter, the next foursome, the guys in the bar. (And lest you think I'm paranoid, let me assure you they ARE watching, because that's what my friends and I do when the situation is reversed, humiliation being sort of a golfing tradition.)

So you address the ball and immediately your brain starts jabbering: "Hit this shot into the water and you'll be a laughingstock. They'll be calling you Captain Hook or, worse, Mulligan Man." This puts your body into a panic, which naturally makes it tense up, which naturally results in a wet ball, or, sometimes, a whiffed ball, which is bad but not as bad as a wet ball because at least with a whiffed ball you can claim it was merely a realistic-looking practice swing.

Golf, like many of life's endeavors, is a game best played brainless.

I have always had particular trouble being watched by anyone other than the people with whom I am playing.

I was in Florida once and the pro shop attendant said, "Just so's you know, there's a big gator named Edgar who suns hisself right behind the teebox on number 7, but he won't bother you unless."

"Unless what?" I asked.

"Unless he ain't eaten lately," he said, laughing.

I figured he was kidding me, but when I got to 7, sure enough there was Edgar, right where the attendant said he'd be, about 30 yards behind the teebox sunning himself with his eyes seemingly closed and that weird semi-smile gators always have on their faces.

He looked full, but we weren't about to risk a leg on our gator-judging abilities. So we hastily teed off from our carts polo-style and lived to tell the tale.

Pressure. It's why I think we ought not be so hard on our golfing presidents. I'd like to see your average amateur bowler roll a strike with a crowd of strangers watching and waiting to giggle. Or how about a city league softballer hitting a home run with a bunch of reporters in stands waiting to tell the world what a boob he is if instead he hits a dribbler to third?

Could they do it? Doubtful, which is why you'll not catch me or my fellow golfers scoffing at the wayward shots of hackers Bush, Ford and Clinton.

Been there, guys. Done that.

— February 23, 1995

How sporting is the game of golf?

I was watching golf on television when the woman with whom I share a toothpaste tube entered the room, glanced at the screen, then sat down and began watching.

You do not know her, so let me assure you that this was highly irregular behavior. She would much rather do ridiculous female things, such as talk about relationships or read a book than watch sports on TV.

But there she sat, raptly watching as putters putted and golfers tipped their caps and mouthed silent thank yous to fans who applauded politely.

After several moments I couldn't take it any longer and I blurted, "Do you feel all right? Should I dial 911?"

"Don't be ridiculous," she replied. "I'm just watching TV."

"But this is golf."

"I can see that."

"But golf is a sport. And aren't you the one who once said you'd rather pull out your eyelashes with pliers than watch sports on TV?"

"Yes, but this is different."

"How so?"

"Well, for one thing there's no fighting, yelling or tantrum-throwing like there is in other sports. In fact, it seems kind of peaceful. All that green, all that quiet. It seems almost pastoral."

Peaceful? Pastoral? Golf? Maybe on the professional level, I explained. But not in real life.

In real life, golf is a leading cause of male stress. In fact, if anyone studied the matter, I'm sure they'd discover that golf is not only a root cause of high blood pressure and heart attacks, but of male pattern baldness and the heartbreak of psoriasis as well.

"But it's just a game," she said. "How could it be so stressful?"

Oh, the innocent.

Golf, I said, is a game designed by the devil himself to drive men mad.

"But that's ridiculous," she said. "I know plenty of women who play. None of them has ever said it's so awful."

Ah, I said, but that's only because women, like they do with so many things, fail to have the proper attitude about golf. To women, golf is a game. They play it, then forget about it.

Many men are incapable of this. To them, golf is an obsession. Their egos tell them they must play it well, and yet they can't because playing good golf is a goal attained only by the aliens on the PGA tour. And this leads to frustration, which leads to the aforementioned medical maladies. And that, I said, is why golf is anything but peaceful or pastoral.

"You're kidding, right?," she said.

Not at all, I replied. For instance, in real-world golf it's a good idea to wear a helmet to protect yourself from all the flying clubs.

"Men throw their clubs?"

Yes, I said. All the time. It's our way of saying, "Oh, pooh, I mis-hit that last shot." My personal best, in fact, is 50 yards, which, incidentally, is 30 yards farther than my shot traveled.

I played with a guy once who helicoptered a club into the branches of a tree. So he threw another club up to knock the first one down, and it became stuck, too.

So he threw a ball to dislodge the clubs, but he missed and the ball hit a lower branch, fell down and clunked him on the forehead. Finally, he shook the trunk of the tree. Naturally, the clubs fell on him and gave him a shiner. He kept playing, but was so shaken he took a 7 or an 8 on every hole. We visit him at the sanitarium often.

"How can guys be so intense about a game?" she said.

I don't know, I said. But we are. I've heard preachers use the Lord's name in vain over duffed chips. I've seen clubs wrapped around trees. I've seen men fall to their knees and weep over missed 6-inch putts. I even know a guy who tossed his bag, clubs and all, into a pond after drowning three straight balls.

My wife, the nongolfer, shook her head.

"That's so pathetic. If golf is so impossible, why play the dumb game?"

I rolled my eyes.

Because it's so relaxing, of course.

— July 27, 1995

Me, Myself and I

My porch, my place, all summer

I'd say it's, oh, 14 feet long and 8 feet wide. It hangs out there on the front of our house like a pooched-out lip, low and droopy.

Except this lip is covered with fluorescent green indoor-outdoor carpet that has running beneath it a mysterious groundhog-like ridge, which, if I am absent-minded enough to place my lawn chair upon, causes me to wobble side to side like the eyes of those grinning cat clocks. Then I have to move by holding tight to the arms of the chair and wiggle-jumping in my seat until I've maneuvered onto steadier ground.

As porches go, I'm afraid it's not very impressive at all. Yet there's where I'll spend my summer. Or at least the happiest hours of it.

Come warm weather, many people opt for the lakeshore to indulge their appetite for a moment's peace, a few seconds of solace. Others prefer the deep woods.

Me? I'll take a porch anytime. Doesn't matter much what kind, either. In fact, the first porch of my adult life wasn't a porch at all. It was the flat roof over a bad deep-fry restaurant in Traverse City, over which I had a small, gloomy apartment.

Late in the evening, with the summer sky turned the color of a bruise and a warm lake breeze dissipating the yellow-fat smell of frying chicken from down below, I would climb out there alone and watch, just watch, like a gargoyle on a shadowy second-story perch, the proceedings below.

Often walkaways from the nearby psychiatric hospital would shamble by, muttering to themselves, dancers to the aimless beat of a demanding rhythm only they knew.

Sometimes there were giggling young lovers, all clasped hands and swinging arms. Or there were loud, angry drunks from the bar down the block, bellowing and cursing to companions or the sky about whatever it was that caused them to drink so much in the first place.

Other times it was so quiet I could hear the traffic light change. A soft click. Did you know they do that?

I watched it all. Or I watched nothing at all. It didn't matter. If the actors didn't show up, I was content to gaze at the stage.

Porches are like that. I am drawn to them. I can sit upon them for hours and hours, with neither a thought in my head nor a need to communicate.

I don't need a reason to be there. The whisper of the breeze against the leaves is enough. Like blush on a woman's cheek, the chance to watch passing people, to glimpse a skulking cat or birds fighting over a nest, to observe whatever or whomever chooses to pass my way, only enhances the appeal, only strengthens the bewitching spell of my creaky old porch.

These days I live in a quiet, family neighborhood with curvy, tree-lined streets. It's wonderful for porch-sitting.

Most of the homes were built when folks had time for such things, a time before TV, and so the porches are long and broad. (Although I notice a few people have screened or glassed them in, which, to me, seems utterly contrary to the point.)

I like to sit out best in the mid- to late evening, when twilight begins to mute the harshness of things and people are in an agreeable humor. It's a magical time.

Sometimes I try to read. Sometimes I let the dog out with me, and we'll sit together, and I'll be amused by his alertness, his nose quivering with the smells of the approaching night.

On very rare occasions, I'll bring out my guitar or harmonica and strum or blow softly. The noise, though, usually seems inappropriate. Porches, by nature, are for quiet times.

People wander by. I nod. I say hello. Most of them I don't

know, but we've got a relationship just the same. They are regular walkers; I am a regular sitter. We each have our roles.

What pleases me most, though, are the times when night has finally fallen, and I look out across the neighborhood and see a tiny dot of light.

It's the glow of a cigarette in the darkness, and it tells me that someone is out there, on his or her porch, doing the same thing that I am, which is nothing, really.

This pleases me. I don't know why, but it does.

And so I smile and kick my feet up on the railing. Then, idly, I watch the glow as it brightens and dims, brightens and dims, until at last it fades into the night, and I am once again all alone.

— June 7, 1990

Please take silliness seriously

Silliness, I think, is vastly underrated. It was an act of silliness, in fact, that recently helped me feel, at long last, a certain kinship with my wife's family.

How it began, I don't know. One moment, 14 of us – my wife's grandparents, her parents, their children and their spouses, all seemingly dignified adults – were seated around a long table at a fancy restaurant chatting quietly.

The next moment a discussion had broken out about tongue curling, who could and who couldn't.

Naturally, everyone had to see if they possessed this vital talent, which caused one of the couldn't-do-its to defend his honor by blurting, "OK, but can you do THIS?" Whereupon he flashed the famous Vulcan "live long and prosper" sign – two fingers left, two fingers right – popularized by Star Trek's Mr. Spock.

Then, of course, we came unglued: Who couldn't whistle; who could wiggle his ears; who could arch one eyebrow (my particular talent); who could tie a cherry stem into a knot with his or her tongue, like the woman on "Twin Peaks." And so on.

We were truly a ridiculous sight. And while the wait staff probably didn't think we were all that hysterical (hey, we stopped short of armpit noises, whatta they want?), we sure did, all except for my wife's grandfather, who doesn't hear so well anymore.

He sat there bewildered, saying, "Huh? What?" every few seconds as he watched his heretofore sane family go mad all around him.

I sat there, gazing at my wife's family, my sides aching with laughter, thinking, "Wow, this is neat." And ever since I've felt something I hadn't felt before around them – a certain closeness with them all.

Ridiculous, right – closer families through goofy facial expressions.

If that's all it took, there'd be self-help books on cherry stem tying in every bookstore and eyebrow-arching experts on "Oprah."

But I've been thinking about this, and here's what I've come up with: To be silly is to let down your guard. To let down your guard is to communicate and to share. And to communicate is to build both relationships and memories.

I should have figured this out years ago. I come from a large and profoundly silly family.

My father used to tell the most awful puns, which, of course, are the best kind. Woe to the child, for instance, who off-handedly mentioned at the dinner table the need for a new pair of shoes.

"You must feel like a real heel for wearing them out," my father would say, a twinkle in his eye.

We six children and our mother would groan, but just as surely one of us would add, with a grin, "Yeah, he's got no sole."

And then we'd be off, a chain of fools adding links to a chain of puns. Heels. Soles. Tongues. Laces. Eyes. Name a shoe part and we'd find a use for it. By the time the chain was broken, we were exhausted by giggles.

This is the kind of place my home was. We were not a joy buzzer family, the kind that passes out that back-of-the-comic-book chewing gum to watch one another's teeth turn black, although I do remember a few items of that ilk around the house.

We were more, and still are I guess, a family of whimsy.

My father is the King of Whimsy. To this day, he has a piece of half-eaten toast, snatched off the plate of Detroit Tigers shortstop Alan Trammell, hanging on the wall of his den, preserved for posterity in a plastic baggie.

Why? I don't know. But I like the idea of it. Why? I don't know. That's just the way we were raised. Silly rubs off on you, and its stain is indelible.

Fine by me.

I enjoy silly. I keep on my desk at work a Squoosh Ball, a poseable Superman, a Kermit the Frog doll, Silly Putty, an empty bottle of dry beer (don't ask) and a plastic cucumber (REALLY, don't ask).

These things seem to make work a little more palatable. They are my spoonful of sugar, as Mary Poppins, another silly person at heart, would say.

And that's why if you come to my house, one of the first things you'll notice, I promise, is a life-sized cardboard cutout of a baby, posed as if crawling across the carpet.

It's a gift – a hint, actually – from my in-laws, and it's utterly silly.

I like that.

When I look at it, I smile. That's the power of things silly. They remind me from where it is that I come, and to not be too serious on the way to where I'm going.

That's important, I think. It's hard enough to get by these days without possessing a keen sense of the absurd.

Not to mention the ability to curl your tongue.

— October 22, 1990

Seeing life all around a blessing

It is true, I never assisted the sun materially in his rising; but, doubt not, it was of the last importance only to be present at it.

– Henry David Thoreau

I am waiting for the dawn. Daylight-saving time has just begun and the clocks have sprung forward, but I have not, and so I am afflicted with that strange pre-dawn alertness that comes to those whose bodies can't tell time according to federal law.

At least they picked a nice morning for it. It is warm, unseasonably so, and I am perched on a flimsy lawn chair on my porch, feet up on the railing. I am dressed in shorts and a cotton Mexican pullover. No shoes.

Strange attire for a concert, but the birds don't seem to mind. They play for themselves and I have a front-row-center seat.

And a one, and a two ...

"Byew byew byew!" one cries as the curtain of darkness rises and the first light begins to spill like a pale red tide over and around the homes across the street.

"Whit whit whit!" sounds another, like the chittering of a bug.

"Awooooo ... hoo hoo hoo," whispers still another. It's a breathy sound, deep and airy. An owl, I think.

But I am not sure.

It occurs to me, suddenly, that I do not know the names of the birds that sing for me. Just as I cannot listen to an orchestra and say for sure which sound is made by the viola, I cannot listen to the birds and say with any certainty, "That is a robin" or "That is a sparrow."

How strange. I grew up in the Upper Peninsula, an outdoorsman's paradise. I should be able to do this. Yet I can't. I was not a child of nature. I was always too busy with indoor things to pay much attention.

This is slowly changing as I grow older. I have taken to swallowing the sights, sounds and smells of the outdoors as a tonic for the stress of the workaday world. I am now the occasional tramper of woods, a sometimes watcher of seascapes. I find myself seeking even small moments outside, like this one.

But still, I do not know the names of things. I cannot look at the trees across the street, whose twisting branches, in their current budless state, look like wild, frozen strands of black spaghetti, and say, "That is an oak" or "There is a maple."

I find that sad. In a sense I have been a foreigner in my own land, especially when it comes to the dawn.

Being a night person, I have seen a grand total of perhaps three dozen sunrises over the course of my life.

Dusk has always attracted me more, when the light dims and the sky changes from blue to purple to black, like a deepening bruise. Dusk is the world's motor shutting down. It is a cooling, peaceful time. I have always loved it.

Yet sitting here watching the light steal like a slow-motion thief over my neighborhood, I cannot imagine what ever convinced me that sleep was more important than this?

And, like so many other chances missed, it reminds me how much we lose by sleepwalking through life, by not thinking to step outside our normal, often deadening routines.

But not today. Today I am awake (in several senses). Today I am watching the eerie beauty of a day's birth, a time when the world still belongs to the creatures and I, on my porch, am only a guest, an observer.

I watch as the birds, mad with pleasure over the coming of

spring, dip and wheel through the warming air. I watch as two squirrels play tag in the tree across the street, a maple, I think.

And I listen as a raven — a black, foreboding wing on the wind — races about bellowing at the top of its lungs, like a neighborhood doomsday prophet: All is lost! The world is ending! Oh, woe! Oh, woe!

But, of course, he is wrong. The world is not ending.

Spring is here, and for some of us the world, like the day, is just now beginning to dawn.

— April 18, 1991

Wise words going out to young cats

Long ago when I was just starting out, I had an editor named Bill McCulloch.

He was a good man and a good editor. But most of all I liked him because long before normal life roped him in he played guitar in bars in Chicago under the name Windy City Slim, which I felt was an extremely romantic thing to do.

God, how I looked up to him. I figured a former musician must know all there is to know about life, so when he waxed philosophic, as was his wont once he'd had a few beers at the bar after work, I listened closely.

Once he said, "Son, you're going to change more in your 20s than at any other time in your life."

I've been thinking about that lately because of a television show on the Fox Network called "Melrose Place."

I have not seen it, nor do I plan to, as I understand it is stuffed with handsome, well-off Californians, all in their 20s, who wear marvelously hip clothing and have nice haircuts.

This is not the sort of stuff I can relate to, growing up as I did a skinny, working-class Michigan boy with a bad haircut and dangerously unhip clothes.

I shudder to think teen-agers will accept "Melrose Place" as evidence of what awaits them in their 20s. From the perch of 31, I think I can provide a more realistic view of what to expect.

Here, then, are a few things I learned in my 20s:

• My parents were not as dumb as I thought. I was not nearly as smart.

• A manual transmission may be cooler, but an automatic saves you a lot of legwork in a traffic jam.

• Don't listen to anyone who says, "That's impossible."

• Priceless are those who don't say, "I told you so," after they told you something was impossible and you went ahead and did it anyway.

• You do not have to shampoo, rinse, then "repeat," no matter what the shampoo bottle says.

• Complaining is useless. Not complaining is hard.

• If you cut a slit in the neck of a banana, the tip won't squash when you begin to peel it.

• Life is like a bad road: avoid dips at all costs.

• It's a pain, but ultimately easier, if you try on clothes at the store.

• Fake it until you know it. Everyone does but no one admits it.

• Don't make any major life decisions in your 20s. You are too stupid. Wait until you are in your 30s, at which point you will be wise enough to realize you are far too stupid to make any major life decisions until you are in your 40s.

• The Peter Principle and Murphy's Law really exist.

• Nothing is as easy as it looks. Nor is anything as hard.

• Fear is the mind-killer. Conquer it and you conquer all. (OK, I picked this up from the book "Dune," but I like it anyway.)

• TV is also a mind-killer. Like most things in life, it's better if taken in small doses.

• Pay attention to the whispers of your soul. Trust them as you would a map, because that's what they are.

• Fiber, fiber, fiber.

• Adulthood stinks. I mean, who decided that adults don't get the summer off?

• Adulthood is the greatest. There ain't nothin' finer than cruising down the road in a car you bought yourself, with someone you love in the passenger seat and the Doobie Brothers' greatest hits on the tape deck.

• By the time you're old enough to buy your own Nintendo, you don't want one.

• If you've made mistakes, remember these words from James Taylor: "Don't assume that the life you left is the life you have to lead."

• Socks are optional. Flossing isn't.

• Marriage is tougher and more rewarding than you could ever imagine. Approach it as you would an unfamiliar dog: slowly and with caution.

• Righty-tighty, lefty-loosey.

• Take the tissues out of your pants pockets before tossing them in the hamper, especially if you don't do the wash. Trust me on this.

• Never order Mexican in anything but a Mexican restaurant.

• There's no such thing as an overnight success.

• Some things in life defy explanation: ice fishing, Geraldo, brussels sprouts, heavy metal, Spam and bosses.

• It's not a good idea to eat a large pizza all by yourself then go on the Tilt-a-Whirl.

• Most of all: Forgive and forget. It's the only way.

Thanks, Slim.

You were right.

— *October 5, 1992*

UFO reports put fun back in adulthood

Long, long ago in a land far away for a very brief moment on a moonlit night, I thought I saw an alien spaceship.

I was on the beach on Aronson Island in Escanaba, my remote little hometown in the Upper Peninsula.

I was watching stars. You can still do that in a town like Escanaba. It doesn't throw up enough light to block the view.

Suddenly there it was, moving fast through the Big Dipper. If I close my eyes now, I can see it. A thin, bright, white light, gobbling great chunks of sky, with a tail as long as a leopard's.

For a brief moment I allowed myself to believe it might be something other than the shooting star I knew it to be.

And in that moment I felt that tickle of excitement that comes when you are confronted by what you think is the mysterious.

To children, the mysterious is commonplace. An animal track in the mud is all the evidence a child needs to believe that Bigfoot roams the woods behind his house. Jackets on bedposts turn nightly into ghosts.

But the older you get, the fewer things carry that tinge of the unknown. You recognize the footprint for a dog's, and fewer things go bump in the night. Bedposts are just bedposts.

I think that's one reason so many of us look longingly back

on childhood. Mystery is for the innocent, something few if any adults can claim to be.

So there on the sand in Escanaba, I indulged. I let the 10-year-old boy in me see what really wasn't there: a silvery, flashing spaceship filled with little green men come to take me away from my routine little life in my routine little town.

It was wonderful. And that's why I choose to believe the recent flurry of reports that have spaceships zipping over our state like fireflies.

On March 8, dozens of people from Grand Rapids to the Lake Michigan shore between Muskegon and South Haven claimed to have spotted large, dark shapes flying low in the night sky.

A Holland family was said to have stared gape-mouthed at a huge, rotating globe with red and white lights hovering just above the trees across the road from their home.

A Holland Sentinel sportswriter (an unimpeachable source if ever there was one) saw a boomerang-shaped grouping of lights flying in formation.

TV stations ran tapes of an excited National Weather Service radar operator reporting something too big to be a plane on his radar, roaring 10 miles across the night sky in 10 seconds:

"It's moving ... and it looks like a big blob. Oh my god, what is that ... now I'm getting three of them ... it's something pretty solid, it's not precipitation or anything ... they look like a triangle on my scope!"

A few days later, a Flint boy spotted a giant, triangular craft hovering directly over his house. "It made a humming sound. And it was big, as big as my whole street," he later told a reporter.

All of this made for great fun. The papers were filled with stories. "Inside Edition" did a report from the Muskegon area. UFO experts flocked in to investigate, leaving behind a trail of intriguing quotes and theories.

I knew it wouldn't last. And I was right. Before long, reporters got around to interviewing "officials." "Officials" are to UFO sightings what wet blankets are to fires.

They said the usual stuff. It was probably a blimp. Or a weather balloon. Or a super-secret military jet or helicopter. Or people were seeing things, maybe even making them up.

A National Weather Service spokesman hastened to explain away its own radar track by saying, "It could have been chaff (metalic foil used by military planes to fool radar detectors) or maybe an airplane."

He was probably right. It was probably chaff, although heaven knows why someone would drop tinfoil over Muskegon. Or maybe it was an airplane. Or a Stealth helicopter. Or the Goodyear blimp. Or a runaway kite.

Flying saucers, in all probability, aren't real, and we are alone in the universe, a tiny planet where bigfoots, Loch Ness monsters and ghosts exist only for children and the young at heart.

But, frankly, I don't want to hear about it.

The experts can talk until they're blue in their way-too-adult faces.

I prefer to believe.

If for no other reason than it's a heckuva lot more fun than not.

— March 27, 1994

Fashion

Fashions no woman would fall for

Bad news, ladies. The fall fashions are in, and once again it's painfully obvious that the people who design your clothes are dangerous lunatics.

I base this statement on the fall fashion magazines. Pick up any one of these magazines, and you will be immediately struck by the fact that you are suddenly having back spasms, fashion magazines being large enough to have their own zip codes these days.

You will also be struck by the fact that very few of the clothes in these magazines resemble something an actual Earth woman would wear in anything but a magazine photo.

Once they finished posing, the models in these photos probably set land speed records sprinting for the nearest dressing room so they could change into normal human clothes before their friends saw them wearing:

•Black fishnet stockings. The New York Times says fishnet stockings are MAJOR fashion news this fall.

"The problem is finding them," an article said. "This racy bit of 1960s redux has taken off like a thoroughbred out of the starting gate."

I'll bet. I'll bet all you women out there can't WAIT to get your hands on a pair of fishnet stockings so you can wear them to the office, right?

You lie. The second you stepped in the door, the other women would set land speed records sprinting for the ladies room, where they would smoke cigarettes and say catty things about whose husband/boyfriend you're after.

The men would simply start chanting, "Whoo! Whoo! Whoo!" the way they do for only two things: 1) touchdowns 2) strippers.

You? You'd take off like a thoroughbred out of the starting gate to go feed your racy bit of 1960s redux through the company shredder.

•Catsuits. The September issue of Vogue (motto: "Seven hundred pages of advertisements plus 14 words!") features photos of women skinny enough to slide through mail slots wearing what look to be body-length longjohns. These are catsuits. The article says they are "practical suits with zippers and pockets, made in nice, sturdy, stretch fabrics. They could be office wear."

On Mars, maybe. Your average woman, though, would almost rather show up naked than wear "sturdy, stretch fabric" to the office. There are two reasons for this:

1) Your average woman has taste.

2) Your average woman – even if she is a beautiful, mature, successful person who weighs 42 pounds – looks in the mirror each morning and sees nothing but Tragic Body Flaws.

This is because women think they should look like fashion models, which is ridiculous because fashion models are all cloned on a secret farm, where they are raised from birth on a special daily diet consisting of three chickpeas and tepid water.

By the way, Vogue says catsuits have a long and glorious history dating way back to, and I quote, the "hard-working gals in the entertainment world: Emma Peel of 'The Avengers,' Catwoman of 'Batman' (and) 'The Jetsons' cartoon characters."

The Jetsons? Just what every woman of the '90s wants to look like: Jane, his wife.

•Plaid. Plaid is HUGE this year. Now, me, personally, I like plaid because I am from the Upper Peninsula, where plaid is the official state color.

However, when you mention plaid to women of non-Yooper descent, they often screw up their faces like they just smelled something bad. This is because, for their entire lives, women have had it drummed into them by the fashion industry that plaid is evil because plaid had horizontal stripes, which, if worn, will make them look like a Scottish version of the Sta-Puf Marshmallow Man.

Now designers have changed their minds. Plaid is suddenly "in" yet nobody knows why.

I figure it this way: One day, Yves St. Laurent was cleaning out his warehouse when he came across several thousand square yards of plaid fabric gathering dust in a corner.

"Sacre bleu!" he said. *"Ow wheel I evair get reed of zees terry-ble fabreek?! ... Wait! Zee fall line! Mon Dieu, I am saved!"*

So he made his entire fall line out of plaid, the other designers followed suit, and the rest is an ugly little slice of fashion history.

Now, some of you might be saying, "But I *hate* plaid. I will just buy something else."

Sorry. This won't do. You cannot fight the fashion industry. Because, frankly, the fashion industry, out of spite, will not MAKE anything else until each and every one of you has purchased your requisite amount of plaid.

Remember shoulder pads?

At one point several years ago, a few women balked at the concept of wearing outfits that made them look as if they had ingested steroids.

So the fashion industry, sensing a mutiny, began putting shoulder pads in everything, until you couldn't buy so much as a tank top without them.

The results were tragic. One evening, my wife, who is all of 5-foot-1, put on a blouse, a blazer and an overcoat, each containing shoulder pads. The result? She looked like a midget linebacker for the Cleveland Browns. Don't tell ME that's not the work of lunatics. I get chills just thinking about it.

Unfortunately, ladies, there doesn't appear to be much you can do about these people. The fashion industry is all-powerful.

If I were you I'd get out there and purchase these fall fashions before I angered the designers and wound up wearing plaid catsuits with black fishnet stockings sewn onto them for the rest of my life.

— September 23, 1991

Reviewing twin cheeks episode

Comes now the indelicate issue of thong bathing suits, popularly known as cheek splitters, hot crossed buns, rope on a dope and several other names entirely too descriptive to mention here.

The state Department of Natural Resources is thinking about outlawing the wearing of such garments at state parks, citing numerous complaints from the visually offended.

But let's slow down a bit. For those of you who, like me, thought thongs were those floppy sandal things you wear to the beach so you don't burn your toes on the sand, let me explain what they really are this way:

If you were to see someone wearing a thong from the front you would say, "Hmm, small bathing suit," but from the back you would say, "Whoa! Full moon to-night!"

Or this way: If you were to lay the posterior of a thong over this column you would still be able to read 98 percent of the words.

Get the picture?

Several months ago Florida legislators did, and they promptly banned the suits on state-owned beaches. The city of Sarasota thought that was such a good idea it outlawed them on city beaches as well.

By the way, I learned about all this by watching "Donahue." You know an issue is of great social significance if it's on "Donahue," as evidenced by his recent provocative piece, "PMS: Real or just a good excuse to be cranky for a week each month?"

So, anyway, Phil had the city fathers of Sarasota on defending the ban. One guy, a big, burly type, kept yammering on about how a legal bathing suit should cover what he kept describing as "the anal cleft."

This mystified the hell out of everybody, including Phil, who has a huge cleft in his chin and was no doubt wondering why anyone would want to wear a bathing suit on his face.

Finally someone in the audience stood up and shouted, "What the heck is an anal cleft, anyway?"

This flustered the big guy, who obviously couldn't think of a polite way to explain what an anal cleft is.

Eventually he gave up and blurted, "IT'S THE CREASE IN YOUR BUTT, OK?!"

Which I thought was pretty funny.

But getting back to the Michigan DNR. I don't think it should ban the suits.

Not that I personally would wear one. They look terribly uncomfortable, plus they bring back some rather unpleasant memories of "wedgies." (If you don't know what a wedgie is, thank your lucky stars because you obviously managed to avoid receiving one back in high school gym class.)

But you should be able to wear one if you want to, a thong that is. This is America, home of the free, land of Demi Moore's pregnancy. Trust me, if we can put up with nude photos of her with a bun in the oven, we can deal with thongs.

Besides, what's the big deal?

First of all, we're all born with the same equipment. What's to be embarrassed about? As Grandma Heller used to tell us kids when we'd get mad at her for barging into our rooms unannounced, "Honey, you ain't got nothing I haven't seen or diapered a thousand times."

Second, it's too difficult to define exactly how wide is not wide enough.

And if the state does define it, are they going to station rangers with tape measures at the gate of all the state parks? If they do, applications to ranger school will increase tenfold, and I'll be the first in line.

Third, if they really want to beautify America's beaches,

they ought to start by banning butt cleavage, thunder thighs and hairy backs.

Or how about guys in Speedos? (Why, why, why is it that every guy who wears these things has a beer gut? Is it a law?) Or women with cottage cheese legs? Or ... don't get me started.

Fourth, it's just a fad. Once people start getting their summer vacation photos back, no matter what shape they're in, they're going to scream, "Oh my god! Are those really my buns or did someone sneak up behind me and tape a couple of seriously overfilled water balloons to my rear?!"

And by next summer they'll be wearing bloomers to the beach.

So to the state DNR, I've got two simple words of advice:

Butt out.

You know, turn the other cheek.

— July 15, 1991

Just give me my Chucks any old day

I am going to write a book someday. It will be called "Confessions of a Tennis Shoe Rebel."

It will be all about how, despite multibillion dollar ad campaigns, I courageously refused to buy into the tennis shoe frenzy of the day.

Incidentally, by saying tennis shoe I do not mean to confuse you. At the ripe old age of 32, I am not so out of it that I do not realize that no one calls tennis shoes tennis shoes anymore, not even tennis players. Nor does anyone call tennis shoes sneakers. Calling tennis shoes sneakers is like calling a couch a davenport or a refrigerator an ice box. Doing so dates you.

Still, we will proceed with "tennis shoes" because I'm the one writing the column. And tennis shoes, I have noticed, like everything else these days, have become specialized.

Tennis players, for instance, wear shoes that are specially designed for tennis. They wouldn't dream of going for a walk in them.

For walking, you need walking shoes, which no self-respecting walker would be caught dead jogging in. They might damage their shoes' special hyperflex, air-flow, foot-cushioning systems. Otherwise known as "heels."

How specialized are athletic shoes? There is even a specific type of shoe for doing general stuff. They're called "cross-trainers." I'm sure they work great, but to me they sound like the type of footwear J. Edgar Hoover wore when the other agents weren't around.

I prefer simpler stuff. At the moment I am wearing a pair of 2-year-old Etonics, also known as "the brand for people with flat feet."

In my closet at home, I have three pairs of Converse Chucks. Remember Chucks? They were the original basketball shoes. And they consisted of two ingredients: canvas and rubber.

They still make them that way. They wear well, they're comfortable and they only cost about 20 bucks. The only problem with them is they seem to be in danger of becoming trendy, which means I may have to dump them, as I am a devout nontrendsetter.

I hope it doesn't come to that. I've seen what else is out there, and I don't like it. For starters, I can't see myself in those shoes where the heel lights up every time you step. Shoes should not need batteries.

Plus, if I ever stop writing columns and do something honest for a living, such as robbing houses, they wouldn't be very practical. I saw a news story recently about a thief who was wearing lighted shoes. The police tracked him through the woods at night by watching his heels. When they caught him, the thief asked how they did it. The police officer, quoting a TV ad, said "It's the shoes. It's gotta be the shoes."

Then there are those pump shoes. When those came out, I thought Reebok was kidding. And I still think they are. I think they were brainstorming one day at Reebok headquarters when some junior exec, to lighten the mood, said "Say, what if we made inflatable shoes?" And after everyone got done laughing, the president said, "You know, that's just dumb enough to work."

Voila! A bold new marketing concept was born. Next up: gelatin-filled shoes. "Buy the new "Jell-Omatic IIs," spokesman Bill Cosby will say. "The only shoes you can play ball in and then eat for dessert!"

Ludicrous? Never happen? Maybe you haven't seen the latest in high-tech footwear. They're called Shaq Attaq IIIs, so named for basketball behemoth Shaquille O'Neal.

The ad I saw said: "Experience the most highly evolved performance shoe technology on the planet."

My initial reaction was, "No, thanks." I don't want to "experience" shoes. I want to "wear" them.

Second, the shoe comes with a pump. Not the kind built into the shoe, but a doohickey called an "Instapump." You carry it around with you in case you have a flat. And if you forget and leave the pump at home, you simply swing by the air hose down at the gas station. What convenience!

Still, I like to keep an open mind, so I called a shoe store and the clerk there told me a pair of Shaq Attaqs costs $129.99.

"That's a lot of money," I said. "But I guess it's worth it. I've always wanted to jump higher. They will make me jump higher, right?"

"Uh, not really," he said.

"Well, at least they'll improve my jump shot. I've always needed a better jump shot."

"I'm afraid they won't do that either, sir."

"Well, what do they do?" I asked.

"They, uh, support your ankle."

I hung up. For 129 bucks, if my ankles need support I'll take them to a good psychotherapist.

It'll be cheaper. And I'll still have money left over to buy some Chucks.

— April 18, 1994

Fashion geeks on a roll with rubber

Attention, ladies. Your new fashion orders have arrived.

Rubber is in.

Hey, now. Let's not hear any grousing. I don't make the rules. If fashion were up to me, I'd immediately ban tube tops and miniskirts since women seem to like them about as much as they like spike heels, pantyhose and ESPN.

But, like I said, I don't make the rules. That's done by fashion designers in Paris, New York and Los Angeles, otherwise known as Mars, Venus and the Planet Bizarro. And this year, according to an article I just read, they say you have to wear rubber coats, dresses and body suits.

I know, I know. I was dubious at first too. I mean, name me someone who's going to wear rubber.

J. Edgar Hoover? Well, yeah. But he'd have worn Saran Wrap, too. Plus, he's dead. I'm talking about someone actually, you know, alive. Cher? All right, someone normal.

See? You can't. That's because most women, no matter how attractive, tend to gravitate toward clothes that will conceal what they believe to be Tragic Body Flaws. Rubber doesn't do that. Rubber clings. And to be honest, most women don't like women who can do cling. For instance, I took my wife to see "Batman Returns" in which Michelle Pfeiffer wears a slinky, rubber bodysuit. I loved it. The body suit, I mean. (The movie sucked.) All Marcia could say was, "You can just tell she doesn't have kids. If she did, she wouldn't be caught dead in that thing."

So I figured, rubber clothes? No way. Then I read the article, and the designers, I don't know, they just made so much sense. For instance, one said: "People say, 'Oh, rubber, that's so kinky.' But we're like 'Hey, it's a material like wool or cotton.' "

Of course it is! And so functional too! Accompanying the article was a photo of a model wearing a snazzy all-rubber ensemble, including thigh-high boots, a dress and a trench coat. She is standing near a car, holding a gas pump handle in a very suggestive manner, if you know what I mean, and you can just tell what she's thinking. She's thinking, "If anyone lights a match, I'm toast." I'm kidding. She's thinking: "If I spill gas on my skirt, why, I can hose it right off!" Try that with cotton.

You are still apprehensive. You're thinking, "If I wear a rubber body suit, I will look like a big, fat seal and someone may try to club me." You must overcome this fear. Designer Andy Wilkes says rubber only scares you because "rubber is black and black is the color of the night, and people are afraid of the dark."

Wilkes says top celebrities such as Salt N' Pepa, Heather Locklear and Roseanne wear his rubber clothes.

You have to admit these are wonderful fashion role models.

OK, I'm not sure who Salt N' Pepa is – a singing group, I believe.

But Heather Locklear is definitely someone men think you should emulate. In fact, I, personally, have heard many, many men say they wish their wives looked exactly like her. Fashionwise, I mean. And Roseanne. Get outta town! Doesn't *every* woman want to look like her?

No? Quiet down. Of course they do.

What I want you to do – and I believe I speak on behalf of the entire fashion industry here – is to pipe down, get in line and buy your rubber clothes like good fashion sheep.

Oh, and one other thing.

I lied about the tube tops.

— November 28, 1994

Local Stuff

Thanks, Phil, we needed chance to vent

Phil Donahue, awash in a sea of people, pointed his microphone in one last direction Monday, listened patiently to one final remark, the credits rolled, and it was a wrap.

"You were a very civil group," he said to the sweaty crowd in Whiting Auditorium. "No one out there (in TV land) is going to believe this didn't come from your heart."

Or our spleens.

It was that kind of afternoon, a gigantic purging of pent-up emotion, a chance for 2,000 people to have their say about, well, you name it.

They spoke of the movie "Roger & Me" and its raffish maker, Michael Moore. They growled about General Motors and its leaders. They jeered and cheered on topics ranging from car quality to job security. A few even talked of God. And after it was all over, a collective exhale seemed to wash over the Whiting crowd, and an entire town seemed to say, "Thanks, Phil. We needed that."

And we did.

For months, since the release of Moore's movie, Flint has been news. Big, mostly bad, news. Flint residents have seen their city discussed and dissected everywhere, from "Late Night With David Letterman" and the "Tonight Show" to The New York Times and The London Times.

Finally, Monday afternoon, it was their turn: a talk show, a national audience, a white-haired, pink-faced host with an open microphone and, boy, oh boy, were folks ready.

They called out to Donahue as he raced up and down the aisles like a human pingpong ball. "Back here, Phil, back here!" the people in back would say. "Up here, Phil, up here!" the people in the front would say. One man shouted, "Over here, Phil. We don't watch any of those stupid soaps."

He didn't get on.

But dozens did, and when their chance to speak came, they clutched the outstretched microphone as if they were never going to let it go. What were to be short commentaries at times turned into lengthy monologues.

"Be brief!" Donahue implored during commercials. "Don't take me around the world!"

But some did anyway. They took him around the world and back. But who could blame them? They had waited a long time for this forum.

When Donahue announced last week he was coming to Flint, long lines formed outside Whiting for the free tickets. People camped overnight. They stamped their feet and froze in the chilly January air for hours, all to get – what? – tickets to a talk show?

"Hey, it's a once-in a lifetime thing," said Todd Butcrakos, 23, of Flushing, a University of Michigan-Flint student who passed the long, cold night doing homework and playing handball against the side of a TV truck with friends. "The show's going to give people the opportunity to say what they think."

Louis Foust, 31, of Flint, a laid-off worker at the Chevrolet Truck & Bus plant, waited eight hours for tickets, then lined up again Monday to ensure he got good seats. (Seating was first-come, first-served.)

"There are," he observed, surveying the crowd minutes before the program, "a lot of camera-hungry people here."

And a lot of folks with a lot on their chests. So much so, in fact, that Donahue decided to tape a second program, to air today here and Wednesday in most other markets.

During the first show, the crowd seemed heavily in favor of Moore, who sat on stage gathering thunderous applause.

"We're with you, Mike!" people shouted as Moore criticized GM for moving plants to Mexico.

"Mike for Mayor!" one man huffed as Moore urged the crowd to political action.

During the second show, however, a subtle shift seemed to take place. More people stood and criticized the maverick film maker for humiliating Flint in the national eye, for making millions off their plight, for not telling what they said was the whole truth. Positive comments followed negative. Whispered remarks followed shouted ones. Thoughtful ideas followed the inane. It was that kind of night.

"I was so nervous, I don't know what I said," said Jeanne Heidenreich, 37, of Flint.

As Donahue later described it, the tapings resembled nothing so much as a gigantic town hall meeting. And through it all, there were some unforgettable moments.

The funniest? During a commercial break, a tubby Moore, standing and stretching on stage, suddenly became self-conscious. "I wish I'd started that aerobics program," he said sheepishly.

The angriest? When the wife of a GM executive stood and defended corporate brass by saying they, too, often work late, sometimes past the dinner hour. She was nearly booed from the auditorium.

"At least they've got jobs to come home from," someone crowed.

The cruelest, most unusual? Each time a GM veteran declared his pride at working 20 or 30 years in the plants, someone would yell, "Retire! Retire!"

If nothing else, the comment, nasty and frustrated, was evidence of the emotion in that room.

"It was," Moore said later as he autographed the paycheck of a woman just laid off by GM, "a very intense crowd."

Intense? Yes. It was a crowd needing to scream and shout and boo and rail against what is both happening to and being said about their town.

"One good thing has come out of this," a man stood and declared toward the end of the final show. "It unified the city."

Probably not. But if Phil Donahue's trip here didn't unite Flint's citizenry, it at least allowed it to blow off a little steam.

Thanks, Phil. We needed that.

— *January 30, 1990*

Deaths raise old questions, no answers

The porch is empty now. I am standing on Mason Street on a hot afternoon a few days after the shooting, and I am looking up at the small porch of the red brick duplex where Rhonda Geter, 15, died a week ago on a sultry Sunday evening in a near downtown neighborhood where plywood seems to cover as many windows as glass.

And like many in this bloody city, I am wondering many things:

I wonder what it must have been like to be here that night, to see the long blue or gray sedan roll slowly by, to see the dark barrel poke from the open window, to see the flashes from the muzzle, to hear the cracking reports. Shouts, panic, blood. A young girl dying, two boys wounded.

I wonder about the gunmen's motive. No one knows yet. One story said it was revenge. Another said it was about turf, a grisly message sent about what is whose. Most seem to agree there was no specific target. Just random shooting. But these are just stories. No one really knows.

I wonder what the hell Rhonda – presumably an innocent, a kid who was simply in the wrong place at the wrong time – and the others were doing there in the first place, hanging out on the porch of a suspected crack house?

I wonder what it must be like to be a child and to grow up in a city, a neighborhood, where gangs and drugs and shootings and death are as normal and familiar as trees and ice cream trucks and basketball games.

But mostly I wonder how many more children have to die before we do something?

Dies the child, dies the city.

I heard that once. I never gave it much thought. Now I do. Our children, this town's richest potential resource, its future, are dying at an appalling rate.

What's the number? Thirty murders in Flint this year, many of them little more than kids? How many more have been injured? How many more have witnessed the carnage? How many of our children have family, friends, neighbors who have been victims? If you were a child, how would these things affect you? What's the ultimate toll?

In the movie "Batman," the Joker declares about Gotham City: "This town needs an enema." Flint needs that and more. It needs an answer, but all we have are the same old questions: What? Who? When? How?

After this, the second drive-by shooting in a month, the latest and most popular form of execution in Flint, our politicians puffed themselves out like roosters and crowed, "No more!"

The police chief growled: "The crap in Los Angeles (may have) become a way of life (there), but it's not going to happen here."

The mayor declared that curbing both the drive-by shootings and the gangs – a term our officials suddenly seem to have discovered after years of using such terms as "groups" and "disorganized bands" – would be first priority, tops on the list. More police presence! they promise. More patrols! Something is being done!

I have no doubt they are sincere. And maybe their efforts will have an effect, although I wonder how much of one.

You can arrest all the so-called bad apples you want and more will still follow. Clip the dandelion, but unless you get at the root, violence will continue to sprout. Again and again.

How can it not when the next generation is watching and learning from the one preceding it? For many of our children, youngsters with no future, the streets are their school, crime and violence their education. Straight-A students abound. The bloodshed continues.

After Rhonda Geter died, Benjamin Davis III, president of the Urban Coalition of Greater Flint, spoke urgently of the need to "impact youth in a constructive, positive fashion."

He said: "All entities in the community can help in doing that – addressing root causes, if you will, instead of symptoms."

A parent, Annie Lockett, pleaded for "community parenting and cultural kinship."

They are wise words.

But how do we achieve these things? If the family falls apart, what can a church, a service organization or the government possibly do? It's the same old question. And I certainly have no answer.

I know, though, that searching for one certainly is more important than drawing tourists to AutoWorld or worrying about the state of downtown or whether we have a hockey team.

Yet where do our dollars and our efforts go? To propping up a foundering theme park instead of to the neighborhoods. To seeking a meaningless civic award instead of to community centers for our restless teens. To Water Streets and Hyatts and Windmill Places — well-meaning projects all, but what's left for the children?

None of this is new, of course. This is the inner city. Each time a Rhonda Geter dies, we stir ourselves momentarily, like bees whose nest has been jostled. Change this, change that. We are filled with good intentions.

Then we forget. Until the next time.

But maybe it will be different this time. Perhaps we are stirred and will stay stirred and maybe, finally, we will accomplish something.

Or, perhaps, we will find there really is no solution, that we have already made every reasonable effort.

But as I stand on Mason Street, looking at the little red porch where a little girl died for nothing, I wonder how many more empty porches are in our future and I know we must continue to try.

Dies the child, dies the city.

I believe that now.

— *July 23, 1990*

Psychologist talks Flint out of depression

If I've heard it once, I've heard it a thousand times: Flint stinks. Flint is the armpit of Michigan. Flint has too much this and not enough that. Flint is never going to change. There's no hope. Blah blah blah.

And you may say, "Who cares what Money magazine thinks?"

But I am not talking about Money magazine or CBS News or any of the other media organizations that have celebrated our badness over the past few years.

I'm not even talking about the idiots from NBC who want to make a situation comedy out of our unemployment, as if having no job were funny.

I am talking about us.

I hear those awful, depressing, no-hope-in-sight things from people who live here. Constantly. White, black, rich, poor.

And so I wonder: Are we, as a city, depressed? Not as in the economic sense. We know that. I'm talking psychologically. Do we have the blues? Worse, now that we've shrunk from the gleaming industrial giant we once were to something far less, could it be that we suffer from ... an inferiority complex? And if so, what can we do about it?

Well, we can simply stay depressed. Or we can do what millions of people do each year.

We can go to a psychologist.

"Have a seat," said Dr. J. Edward Chase, gesturing toward a grouping of several chairs and a couch in his small Grand Blanc office.

A couch?

I had sought out Chase for several reasons. One, he lives in Flint and has for years. Two, he's a good sport, so I knew he wouldn't whip out a straitjacket the moment I suggested he treat Flint like a patient.

In fact, he liked the idea.

"I think Flint's very much that way – wallowing in it's own self-pity," he said. "It'll always be depressed as long as it views itself as a victim."

The rules were simple. I would play Flint. He had just this one session to help me – microwave urban psychiatry, as it were.

But first I had to choose a seat. This is not easy to do when you are in a psychologist's office. I looked at the couch. I looked at the chair.

I took the chair. Hey. No way was I going to sit, much less lie, on a couch in a psychologist's office like I was a *crazy* city or something! Hey. Maybe *Detroit* would use the couch, but ...

"The first thing we do," Chase began, "is ask whether this (hopeless view) is an accurate picture of yourself. A lot of people get depressed because they take the attitude of their critics."

Have I done that? he asked.

Let's see. In the past two years, I've been the subject of newspaper articles, magazine pieces, national TV shows and a movie, all of them talking about what a rotten place I am.

Yup. I guess you could say I've taken on the attitude of my critics.

What I need to do, he said, is to "separate my beliefs about myself from those of others."

"There are things you want to improve about yourself, right?" he said.

Right. We could use more jobs, less crime, a better downtown, more jobs. A movie theater in town would be nice. And, oh, yes, more jobs. We could definitely use some more jobs.

"I believe the solutions for problems reside within the individual. The problem is you're pining away for your past glory. It doesn't do any good to just yearn or to believe the critics that good times will never come again.

"Depression grows passivity. If I'm waiting for something to be given to me, it's not going to happen. If you're waiting for GM or the state to rescue you, that's no way to get over your depression. You're putting yourself in the role of the victim, and victims can't help themselves. You have to be active, not reactive. Like a missile, you have to have something to shoot at."

Hmmm. How about AutoWorld? I'd love to fire a missile at that place. And Money magazine. Ha! Love to nuke those suckers. Or how about ...?

"Goals." said Chase. "You need goals."

Specifically, goals that I can "see, smell, taste, touch. Goals have to be sensory-based."

The way to set goals, he added, is to think about times in the past when people came together to solve a problem or fulfill a dream. The College and Cultural Center, for example. That was a major success and certainly no piece of cake to put together.

"Look at how that came together," Chase said. "Was everyone involved? Was everybody behind it? Some were, some weren't. What they probably had was an inspirational leader whose vision was clear enough that others could see it."

Hmmm. I seem to be a wee bit short in the visionary department over at City Hall right now.

"Well, if not (City Hall), it could be a corporation or a civic leader or a volunteer or a kid in the 12th grade. Why not study (cities) that have done it successfully? If one city can do it, why can't you?"

I guess there is Cleveland. It's an industrial city that's started to turn things around. And Lowell, Mass. And Dayton, Ohio. Some say that's becoming a better place.

Once I've identified my goals, Chase continued, I need to identify and set about getting the resources I need to fulfill them. You'd be surprised, he added, how many of those resources can be found from within.

Then it's simply a matter of taking things one step at a time. Or as Chase put it: "If you were to sit down to a seven-course meal, wouldn't you feel overwhelmed if you had to eat it in one bite?"

I guess. Especially if it were a coney with extra onions from Angelo's.

"Put things into chewable chunks. Be persistent and flexible. If something doesn't work, try something else. Successful people see failure as feedback so they can try something else."

Hey. We've got plenty of feedback. Bags and bags of feedback. Especially about downtown. If we could sell all the feedback we've gotten about downtown we'd be rich.

"Remember," he added. "You don't have to buy into what (others) say about you."

Our session was over. Chase promised that if I followed his goal-setting process and stayed "active and assertive" I'd soon find myself on the road to becoming a "happy, well-adjusted city."

Of course, a few more sessions wouldn't hurt, he said.

"I think this particular patient could be out of therapy in a little less than 20 sessions."

Which is reasonable. But I figure if we can't snap out of this funk by then, maybe stronger measures are called for.

Anyone for electro-shock therapy?

— May 13, 1994

Money magazine true to its name

This is going to sound incredible, but I'm beginning to suspect that Money magazine's annual ranking of the nation's 300 largest cities is – you readers with pacemakers might want to stop reading here – *nothing more than a cheap gimmick to make money!*

I know. Crazy, right?

But what else can it be? What else can explain Flint's astonishing improvement this year? On last year's list, we were dog food, the 299th best (or worst) city in the land. The magazine didn't declare us "Slime Pit USA," but they might as well have.

Now, suddenly, we're 213th – "Still a slime pit, but a much nicer one!"

What happened? Did Flint win the lotto when I wasn't looking? Did GM suddenly say to the 10 trillion people it's laid-off here over the past decade, "C'mon back, folks, we were only kidding?"

Or did Disney buy AutoWorld?

I want to know, because unless I missed something, this hasn't exactly been a banner year in Flint history: Water Street closed; "Roger & Me" opened; AutoWorld suffered a flat; the Flint Spirits, RiverFest, downtown fireworks and the air show all faded away; and there haven't been any new Al/Yvonne Bennett commercials in months.

I'm not trying to be a downer. It simply hasn't been a great year, by any measure. And yet we improved. Dramatically. Why?

And how about Grand Rapids? In 1989, the town that makes William F. Buckley look like a flaming liberal was at 198. This year it's 228.

That must have really cheesed off the city fathers over there. I bet they screamed at the city mothers and kicked the city dogs.

But did Grand Rapids really become worse? Didn't I just see a Free Press article about how everyone is planning to move to Grand Rapids because it's so swell? Are these people now going to reconsider, saying, "Whup! Unpack the bags, honey. G.R. fell to 228."

Or how about Bremerton, Wash.? This year it was, according to Money, the best city in America. Last year, though, it was a lowly 179th.

"What's your secret?" I recently asked Louis Mentor, Bremerton's mayor.

"Beats me," was pretty much his response. A new highway's going in, he said, and there's a whole list of public improvement projects planned, and the climate's nice.

But doesn't it rain a lot in Washington? I asked. (Bremerton is near Seattle.)

"Well, yes," he said. "We get half an inch of rain a lot of days, and it takes all day to get it. But that beats tornadoes."

He had a point. I think.

But other than that, it didn't sound like a whole lot had changed in Bremerton in the past year, which is why I'm beginning – just beginning, mind you – to smell a rat.

I think the people at Money realize that if their rankings, which are based on a raft of statistics, from housing to health care, stayed the same from year to year, people would eventually get bored and stop buying that particular issue, which is one of its biggest sellers.

So they add a few statistical categories each year, juggle things around a little bit, and voila!: Lima, Ohio, is suddenly the nation's best. ("The best durn tractor pulls going!")

It's a great gimmick.

The ones on the top have something to put on their city limit signs, for a year at least. The ones on the bottom buy a truckload of the magazine to burn, the way Flint did in 1987 when it was 300th.

Everyone's happy. Or unhappy. But that's the beauty of it. Money magazine wins either way!

Of course, Money won't tell you this.

When I spoke with Richard Eisenberg, author of the article, he said the magazine publishes the rankings because they represent "an interesting snapshot of America."

His explanation for the radical rise/fall some cities make is that statistical categories and the weight assigned each change. (Flint's rank improved this year, he said, because the magazine decided we should get credit for being so near Detroit, which in my mind is sort of like saying Kuwait is a nicer place to live because it's so close to Iraq, but that's another story.)

But my explanation is the magazine's name. Because I wonder how meaningful statistics are. Statistically, Oakland A's outfielder Jose Canseco is a gem. As a human being, though, he's a cubic zirconium. It's that way with towns, too, don't you think? Immeasurables, intangibles count the most?

Of course, this is not to say that we here in Flint are upset at Money. Oh, sure, its survey has treated us like we've had a bad case of urban halitosis for the past four years. But all could be forgiven. Easily. Say, for the top spot on next year's list.

And they can justify it so easily.

Just throw in a category on coney island restaurants per capita or something.

— August 27, 1990

Get digging: Michael Moore is coming

It is Memorial Day and I should be relaxing. But I am not relaxing. I am digging a bomb shelter.

I suggest you do the same. And you'd better hurry. There's not much time. My understanding is Michael Moore's new television program could hit the airwaves any minute, and I, for one, am not taking any chances.

You probably want an explanation.

OK. Michael Moore, Flint's well-known gadfly, is making a television show for NBC called "TV Nation." It's supposed to be a parody of "60 Minutes," with Moore playing the role of Lesley Stahl, only without the dress.

The premise is pretty simple. Moore runs around the world with his camera and pesters people the way he did in "Roger & Me."

For instance, in the first piece, he travels to Mexico for a piece on the free trade agreement ("Tell me, are you forced to sell rabbits to survive?"), to New York for an in-depth look at racist cab drivers ("Tell me, do you have to sell white rabbits to survive?") and to Niagara Falls for an item on the Love Canal ("Tell me, do your rabbits glow?").

The show's last segment is on Flint. You would think Moore would have had enough of making fun of Flint. I mean, what'd we ever do to him?

But no. This time Moore discovers that the former Soviet Union had (and apparently still has) a nuclear missile trained on our fair city.

This is alarming news. This is also puzzling news. Why in the world, I wonder, would anyone want to nuke little old Flint?

Is it because of our auto industry? That would be my first guess. But I doubt a nuclear missile could do any more damage to the auto industry around here than General Motors has already done.

So who or what are they after? Our stealth AutoWorld technology? Our ability to turn paddlewheelers into submarines? Our youthful commandos-in-training down at the MTA bus terminal? What?

After a lot of thought, I can come up with only one solution, one area in which Flint is clearly a world leader and which would therefore make us an attractive target for a foreign power with an itchy nuclear finger.

Coneys.

We make more and better coneys here than anywhere else in the world. That fact is indisputable. Knock out Flint and you knock out a city on the cutting edge of coney island technology.

It's all so clear now. I knew the Soviets, and now the Russians, I suppose, were diabolical, but plotting to knock out a nation's coney capital is despicable.

Not to worry, though. I called Tom Branoff down at the famous Angelo's Coney Island emporium on Davison Road and he assured me that Angelo's has already taken steps to assure that Genesee County's coney supply will not be interrupted in the event of a nuclear attack.

"We got an underground bunker," he said, "We hid our formula down there so we (can) keep the coneys coming."

The idea that the Russians would launch an attack did not surprise him.

"The Soviets want our recipe. The Chinese want our recipe. Everybody wants our recipe."

But Angelo's is prepared. So rest easy.

Now all I have to worry about is myself. I say this because, in his show, Moore reveals that ground zero is the former Chevy plant in the AC Rochester Flint West complex, which is about six blocks from my house.

This is not good news. If a nuclear bomb explodes six

blocks from my house, there's a good chance my wife and I will become french fries.

What's worse news, though, is that, in his piece, Moore travels to the former Soviet Union to convince officials there to tell him where the bomb is stored so he can "disarm" it.

I can see it now.

MOORE: Show me the missile you have aimed at Flint.

OFFICIAL: Nyet!

MOORE: Show me the missile or I will do to you what I did to Roger Smith, Miss Michigan and geeky game show host Bob Eubanks.

OFFICIAL: AIYYYIEEEE!

This is why I am so concerned. I mean, to say Michael Moore is just a little antagonistic is to say that David Koresh was just a little nuts.

So what happens if, after Moore's show hits the boob tube, the Russians get really mad and say, "To hellski with international peace, we're nuking that s.o.b.'s hometown, coneys or no coneys!"?

You have to admit it wouldn't be an unusual way to react to Michael Moore. If Roger Smith had nuclear weapons, Flint would have been toast years ago.

The show airs this summer or fall.

I'd get digging if I were you.

— May 31, 1993

Some words for Japanese to live by

The list is long and sad.

Look out.

Watch out.

Stick 'em up.

They are phrases given to a Japanese exchange student on his way to America, and in their bluntness they tell a better story about what we have allowed ourselves to become than anything else I can think of.

Put your hands up.

Face down.

Duck.

In essence, they are words of survival. Learn us, the words seem to say, and you will understand. Understand and the person shouting them at you may not beat you. Or shoot you. Or arrest you. Understand and you may live.

Go away.

Keep out.

Don't move.

The list came to me from John Davidek, a teacher at Flint Southwestern Academy. It was given to him by a student of his, Tadahide Sato, a shy, slight 17-year-old from Koga City, Japan.

The class had been talking about Takuma Ito and Go Matsuura, the two Japanese college students who were shot to death recently by a carjacker in San Pedro, Calif.

Their fatal mistake was becoming hungry. One night at about 11, they drove to a 24-hour grocery in San Pedro, a peaceful town on the shoulders of the madness in Los Angeles. In the parking lot, two men approached, shot them each in the head, left them to die and stole their car with the bumper sticker on the back that said "I Love N.Y."

Japan was shocked. In a society where private ownership of guns is banned, drugs are few and violence rare, they could not understand. The headlines said, "Gun Society ... Another Tragedy in Los Angeles. For a Car?"

Here in America, President Clinton issued a formal apology to the Japanese people through ambassador Walter Mondale, but, really, to most Americans, the crime was no big deal. Two college kids shot in a two-bit robbery doesn't amount to much in a nation where murderers sometimes eat their victims and drive-by shootings are as common on the news as the weather report.

Some of those in Davidek's class were certainly unimpressed. A straight-A student said, "This thing is blown out of proportion because they're Japanese students. It's just two more bodies in the morgue."

The attitude would shock Davidek if he did not spend his days with youngsters. Today's teens are simply not shocked as easily as the kids who came before them. Violence is commonplace, whether they see it on TV or in the hallway.

That day, in fact, before Davidek's class, two students became involved in a fight. One student got the other down and began kicking him in the head.

Davidek's class talked about it. A girl said the law of the street is that "you do anything to get someone down – anything."

The law of the street. That's the way it is in America these days. We accept it as almost normal, and yet it is not. It is an attitude much of the rest of the world does not understand.

Davidek remembers visiting Osaka, Japan, years ago. He met the mayor and asked him how many murders had occurred in the last 12 months in Japan's third largest city, a city of millions. The mayor replied 27.

"And he apologized for it," Davidek remembers. "He was embarrassed. At the time, 27 murders was a good weekend in Detroit."

The violence here – particularly the Halloween '92 slaying of a Japanese teen in Baton Rouge, La., whose only crime was banging on the door of the wrong house – is what prompted Japanese officials with Youth for Understanding to issue the list to Sata as he headed for our shores.

Hands in front of you.
Hand it over.
Get out-a-here.
I'm serious.
Knock it off.
This is not a game.

Sata says he tried, but has not learned all of the phrases. It is a long list for a teen-ager to learn, filled with American words that are bumpy to the Japanese tongue. He is hoping he will not need them. The only ugliness he's seen so far is a fight inside a Taco Bell. "I like America," he says. "The people are friendly."

And yet he knows it is out there.

"My American friends," he begins, "they say there is a lot of violence."

I wonder. How do you say "God help us" in Japanese?

— April 3, 1994

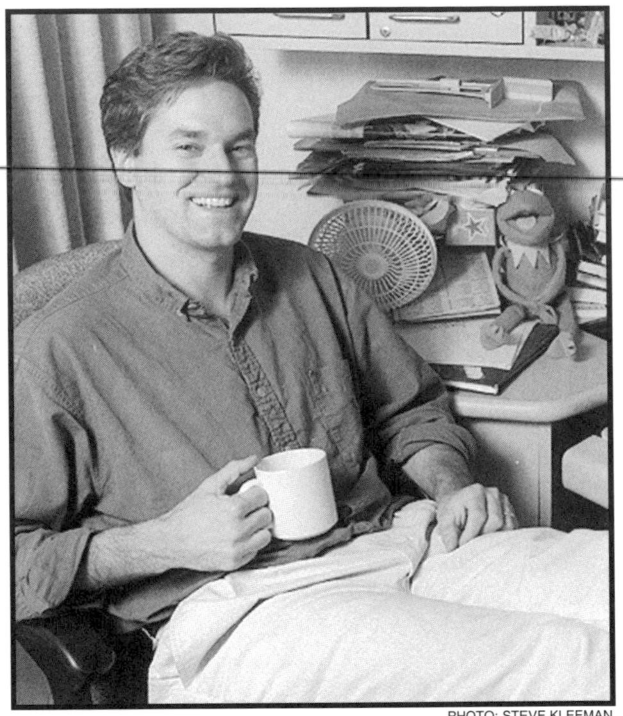

PHOTO: STEVE KLEEMAN

Andrew Heller was born in 1961 in Dearborn and raised in Escanaba. He graduated from Central Michigan University in 1983 and has worked as a columnist for The Flint Journal since 1989. He lives in Grand Blanc Township with his wife, the lovely yet formidable Marcia, and their two children. He enjoys a really good piece of toast.